FINDING THE REAL JESUS

A Guide for Curious Christians
and Skeptical Seekers

Resources by Lee Strobel

The Case for Christ

The Case for Christ audio

The Case for Christ — Student Edition (with Jane Vogel)

The Case for Christ for Kids (with Rob Suggs)

The Case for Christmas

The Case for Christmas audio

The Case for a Creator

The Case for a Creator audio

The Case for a Creator — Student Edition (with Jane Vogel)

The Case for a Creator for Kids (with Rob Suggs)

The Case for Easter

The Case for Faith

The Case for Faith audio

The Case for Faith — Student Edition (with Jane Vogel)

The Case for Faith for Kids (with Rob Suggs)

The Case for the Real Jesus

The Case for the Real Jesus audio

Faith Under Fire, curriculum series

God's Outrageous Claims

God's Outrageous Claims audio

Inside the Mind of Unchurched Harry and Mary

Off My Case for Kids (with Robert Elmer)

Surviving a Spiritual Mismatch in Marriage
(with Leslie Strobel)

Surviving a Spiritual Mismatch in Marriage audio

What Jesus Would Say

FINDING
THE
REAL JESUS

*A Guide for Curious Christians
and Skeptical Seekers*

LEE STROBEL

ZONDERVAN

ZONDERVAN.com/
AUTHORTRACKER
follow your favorite authors

We want to hear from you. Please send your comments about this book to us in care of zreview@zondervan.com. Thank you.

▌ZONDERVAN®

Finding the Real Jesus
Copyright © 2008 by Lee Strobel

Requests for information should be addressed to:

Zondervan, Grand Rapids, Michigan 49530

Library of Congress Cataloging-in-Publication Data

Strobel, Lee, 1952–
        Finding the real Jesus : a guide for curious Christians and
    skeptical seekers / Lee Strobel.
            p.   cm.
        ISBN 978-0-310-28787-2
        1. Jesus Christ — Historicity. 2. Jesus Christ — Biography —
    History and criticism. I. Title.
    BT303.2.S77   2008
    232 — dc22   2008025042

Interior design by Beth Shagene
Editorial assistance by Cassandra Gunn

Printed in the United States of America

---

08 09 10 11 12 • 20 19 18 17 16 15 14 13 12 11 10 9 8 7 6 5 4 3 2 1

·CONTENTS

INTRODUCTION

I first encountered Frank Walus when I was a reporter at the *Chicago Tribune*. Federal prosecutors had revealed to me the startling news that this unassuming Southwest Side resident was actually a Nazi terrorist who had participated in the murder of innocent Jews in Poland during World War II.

They painted a gruesome picture. They said that while he was accompanied by Nazi SS troops, Walus separated children from their parents and then helped shoot the children to death. Later, working with the Gestapo, he allegedly ordered a woman to disrobe in the presence of her two daughters—and when she refused, he shot her to death. The two girls were also killed. In addition, Walus was accused of beating a Jewish prisoner to death with a metal bar at a local Gestapo headquarters.[1]

Prosecutors filed a lawsuit to strip Walus of his U.S. citizenship on grounds that he had concealed his Nazi past when he applied for entry into the country. At his trial, aging witnesses dramatically pointed out Walus as the perpetrator of atrocities in the Polish cities of Kielce and Czestochowa. A federal judge declared the government's charges substantiated, and Walus was ordered to relinquish his citizenship.[2]

It would be tempting, in light of the horrendous

7

image of Walus that emerged at his trial, to join a gang of vigilantes and storm the courthouse demanding swift and severe punishment for this monster. After all, eyewitnesses identified him as a heartless killer and a judge ruled that the case against him had been proven by a preponderance of the evidence. *But not so fast.*

Walus' attorneys offered a far different portrait of him. He wasn't a collaborator with the Nazis, they said. Rather, Walus was a victim himself—trucked to Germany and required to work as a forced laborer on farms in three villages.

They also pointed out that there was no corroborating evidence to back up the eyewitnesses who identified Walus as a Nazi thug. And they cast doubt on whether these witnesses could accurately identify Walus, then in his 50s, based on their memories of what he looked like when they claimed they briefly encountered him as a teenager during the war.

However, it wasn't until after the trial that the true picture of Walus came into sharp focus. His attorney, Charles W. Nixon, found a Red Cross list of forced laborers in Germany during the war, including thirty who were Poles like Walus. Eight of them offered sworn testimony that Walus had been among them.

Then a German priest and two former French prisoners of war confirmed Walus' account. Finally, a German archivist unearthed a copy of Walus' intake working permit issued by the Nazis in 1940—further confirmation of his defense.

In light of these developments, investigators dropped

the entire case against Walus. The new evidence, said a federal judge, "exonerates the defendant of all charges made against him."[3]

"I'm glad the case is over," Walus told the press. "But I lost everything: my reputation, my health. What was done to me was terrible."[4]

In the troubling case of Frank Walus, two diametrically opposed portraits of the same individual were presented. There was testimony to support each one—but the most dramatic picture, though touted by a credible source, evaporated upon closer examination of the surrounding facts.

For Walus, the effects were personally devastating. That's bad enough, but there's even more at stake when we consider the conflicting portraits of Jesus Christ that are being enthusiastically promoted to the public these days.

Increasingly, the traditional picture of Jesus is under an intellectual onslaught from critical scholars, popular historians, TV documentaries, bestselling authors, Internet bloggers, Muslim debaters, and atheist think tanks. They're capturing the public's imagination with dramatic new depictions of Jesus that bear scant resemblance to the picture historically embraced by the church.

But if there's any lesson from the horror that Frank Walus endured, it's that a surface-level consideration of the facts is simply not enough. When we're dealing with a topic as important as the identity of Jesus, we need to go beyond opinion, speculation, and hype in order to find the solid ground of historical evidence. In the end, which portrait would prove to be the most accurate?

Personally, I felt a sense of urgency to investigate these issues. After all, these provocative portrayals of Jesus have confused many spiritual seekers who are on a personal quest for the truth about him. And in some cases, they are even sending Christians into a tailspin of doubt—a stomach-churning experience that I have suffered first-hand.

Who Is the Real Jesus?

As I've described in earlier books, I was a spiritual skeptic until my wife became a Christian in 1979. Impressed by the changes in her character and values, I decided to use my journalism and legal training to systematically investigate whether there's any credibility to Christianity—or any other faith, for that matter. After nearly two years, I concluded that the scientific data point powerfully toward the existence of a Creator and that the historical evidence for the resurrection establishes convincingly that Jesus is divine.[5]

But now let me tell you the rest of the story:

As a new Christian, I volunteered at my church to respond to questions submitted by people attending the weekend services. One Sunday I got a card from a twelve-year-old girl who said she simply wanted to know more about Jesus. When I called her, she asked if my wife and I could come over for dinner with her and her dad.

"Aw, isn't that cute?" I said to Leslie. "This is gonna be fun!"

When her father opened the door, I walked in and glanced at the coffee table in the living room. Sitting there were stacks of heavyweight books. It turns out her dad was a scientist who had spent years studying articles and books attacking the traditional portrait of Jesus.

For hours over pizza and soft drinks, he peppered me with tough objections, some of which I had never even considered during my investigation of Christianity. Tremors rippled through my faith. In fact, my head was starting to spin! I felt what I call "spiritual vertigo"—that queasy sense of dizziness and disorientation that courses through the body when someone challenges the core of your faith in a way that you cannot answer.

A chill went down my spine. *Maybe he's right! Maybe I didn't ask all the right questions. Maybe I swallowed this Christianity thing hook, line, and sinker without adequately checking it out.*

Have you ever felt spiritual vertigo? Here's my prediction: if you haven't, you probably will—and soon, because the challenges to the traditional understanding of Jesus are coming fast and furious.

Did you know, for example, that the church suppressed alternative gospels that present Jesus in an entirely different light than the Bible? Or that the New Testament is so hopelessly riddled with errors that it can't be trusted? Or that Jesus failed to fulfill the messianic prophecies? Or that Jesus never really died on the cross or rose from the dead?

If you're a Christian, what are you going to do when your son, daughter, neighbor, or colleague encounters one of these allegations and peppers you with questions? Or if you're a spiritual seeker, how do you know that the picture of Jesus you're encountering on the Internet or hearing about from college professors is really an accurate portrayal of him?

In other words, who is the *real* Jesus? For two millennia, the portrait of Christ painted by the church has been the *divine* Jesus — the God who became a man. That's what we celebrate at Christmas: God incarnate. As the apostle Paul put it, "He is the image of the invisible God."[6] The apostle John was more poetic: "In the beginning was the Word, and the Word was with God, and the Word was God.... The Word became flesh and made his dwelling among us."[7] But now critics are painting Jesus far differently. For instance, there's:

- The *Gnostic* Jesus, who's a purveyor of secret wisdom rather than the redeemer of humankind;
- The *misquoted* Jesus, whose story in the Bible is so pockmarked with errors that it can't be trusted;
- The *failed* Jesus, who never fulfilled the messianic prophecies;
- The *uncrucified* Jesus, who never died on the cross for anyone's sins;
- The *deceased* Jesus, who never proved his divinity by rising from the tomb.

Some of the arguments that are offered in favor of

these new portraits sound quite persuasive. That's why spiritual vertigo can strike. But Proverbs 18:17 makes this astute observation: "The first to speak in court sounds right, *until the cross-examination begins.*"[8] In other words, the picture can change dramatically when you hear the other side of the story.

Just ask Frank Walus.

So why don't you come along with me on my journey of discovery? I'll be traveling from Los Angeles to Charlotte and from Dallas to Halifax to confront scholars with these latest claims about Jesus. Actually, this is the kind of quest that the Bible invites. "Test everything," urged the apostle Paul. "Hold on to the good."[9]

Let's resolve at the outset to keep an open mind and follow the facts wherever they take us — even if it's to a conclusion that challenges us on the deepest levels. In the end, we'll discover whether the traditional portrait of Jesus is the genuine article with infinite value, or a cheap fake that should be relegated to the trash bin of history.

CHAPTER 1

PORTRAIT #1:
THE GNOSTIC JESUS

Is He a Purveyor of Secret Wisdom
or Redeemer of the World?

The documents in the New Testament offer a very distinct picture of Jesus: He's the resurrected Son of God who redeemed humankind through his atoning death on the cross.

Yet those aren't the only texts from ancient history. Several so-called Gnostic gospels unearthed in the twentieth century, including the Gospel of Thomas, portray Jesus far differently. This isn't a matter of merely adding some new brush strokes or shading to the traditional portrait of Jesus; instead, it's an entirely different canvas and a whole new likeness.

Although Gnosticism is diverse, New Testament scholar N. T. Wright says Gnostics historically have held four basic ideas in common: the world is evil, it was the product of an evil creator, salvation consists of being rescued from it, and the rescue comes through secret knowledge, or *gnosis* in Greek.[1]

"What is needed," says Wright, "is a 'revealer' who will come from the realms beyond, from the pure upper spiritual world, to reveal to the chosen few that they have within themselves the spark of light, the divine identity hidden deep within...."[2]

For many Gnostics, that revealer is Jesus of Nazareth, who in their view isn't the savior who died for the sins of the world, but rather is the imparter of secret wisdom who divulges the truth about the divine nature within each of us.

The contrast between the biblical and Gnostic Jesus is stark when the gospels of John and Thomas are compared. "John says that we can experience God only through the divine light embodied in Jesus," said Princeton religion professor Elaine Pagels. "But certain passages in Thomas' gospel draw a quite different conclusion: that the divine light Jesus embodied is shared by humanity, since we are all made in the image of God."[3]

While John stresses the resurrection as evidence of Jesus' divinity, "Gnostic writers tend to view ... the resurrection and other elements of the Jesus story not as literal, historical events but as symbolic keys to a 'higher' understanding," said religion writer Jay Tolson.[4]

In addition, the salvation offered in Thomas is at odds with biblical accounts. While the Bible stresses that forgiveness and eternal life are freely available to everyone who receives them in repentance and faith, in the Gnostic view "a person has to be worthy to receive Jesus' secret wisdom," said Ben Witherington III of Asbury Theological Seminary.[5]

Again contradicting the New Testament, Thomas quotes Jesus as telling his disciples: "If you fast, you will bring sin upon yourselves, and if you pray, you will be condemned, and if you give to charity, you will harm your spirits." And contrary to the Bible's depiction of Jesus as elevating the lowly status of women, he is quoted in Thomas as teaching that "every female who makes herself male will enter the kingdom of Heaven."[6]

Canada has already seen the birth of its first Gnostic church.[7] In the United States, "there is a growing, if disconnected and unorganized, Gnostic movement," said Richard Cimino and Don Lattin in their survey of American spirituality.[8] "The Gnostic factor can be found in the growth of occult and esoteric teachings and movements, where access to supernatural secrets are available through individual initiation and experience rather than through publicly revealed texts or doctrine," they said.[9]

So which picture of Jesus is true? Is he the one-and-only Son of God, or is he "an avatar or voice of the oversoul sent to teach humans to find the sacred spark within"?[10] At the heart of this controversy is the reliability of the Gnostic gospels that have been uncovered over the past six decades. Do they tell a more accurate story about Jesus than the New Testament?

To get answers, I flew to Nova Scotia, Canada, to interview a New Testament historian who is respected by liberals and conservatives alike. Craig A. Evans came to Acadia University in 2002 after spending more than twenty years as a professor at Trinity Western University, where he founded the Dead Sea Scrolls Institute. He received his doctorate in biblical studies from Claremont Graduate University and has written or edited more than fifty books, including *Fabricating Jesus: How Modern Scholars Distort the Gospels*.[11]

Evaluating Ancient Documents

I asked Evans to set forth the criteria that historians use in determining whether an ancient text is reliable.

"The first question is, 'When was it written?'" he said. "If the document is about Alexander the Great, was it written during the lifetime of those who knew him? Same with the New Testament. There's a huge difference between a gospel written in AD 60 — about thirty years after Jesus' ministry — and another document written in AD 150.

"If the Gospel of Mark was written in the 60s, then it was written within the lifetime of numerous people who would have known Jesus and heard him teach. This would have a corrective effect. But if a document is written sixty, eighty, or a hundred years later, then that chain is lost. Although it's not impossible that a document written much, much later could contain authentic material, it's a lot more problematic.

"A second issue," he continued, "involves a geographic connection. For example, a document written in the Eastern Mediterranean world thirty years after Jesus' ministry is more promising than one written in Spain or France in the middle of the second century.

"A third issue involves the cultural accuracy of the document, in terms of its allusions to contemporary politics or events. This can expose phony documents that claim to have been written earlier than they really were. When we have a writer in the second or third century who's claiming to be recounting something Jesus did, often he doesn't know the correct details.

"Then there are motivational questions. Did the writer have an axe to grind? We look at the New Testament documents and, yes, they have an agenda: they're affirming that Jesus is the Messiah, the Son of God. But they also make all kinds of statements that can be evaluated. Are they culturally accurate? Are they true to what we know from other historical sources? Were they written in a time and place that has proximity to Jesus' life? The answers are yes.

"When we get into other gospels, the answers to those questions are almost always no. They're written in a later period of time—too late to be historically reliable. They're written from other places with strange and alien contexts. We find inaccuracies at key points. We can see they're derived from earlier sources. Sometimes there's a philosophy, like Gnosticism, that's being promoted."

Christianity or Christianities

"Some scholars give these other gospels very early dates of origin," I said. "This backs up their claim that first-century Christianity featured a broad range of differing doctrines—all equally legitimate—and the more powerful orthodox wing crushed these other valid Christian movements. Is it true that the earliest Christianity was a fluid melting pot of different perspectives about Jesus?"

"It's not true at all," Evans insisted. "This is the product of a modern agenda—a politically correct, multicultural agenda motivated by sympathy for marginalized groups. The question is: What really did happen in the first century? What are the facts?"

I jumped in. "What *are* the facts?" I asked.

"Well, the early Christian movement certainly did have disagreements over this and that. But there weren't 'Christianities.' There wasn't one Christianity that thought Jesus was the Messiah and another Christianity that didn't; another Christianity that thought he was divine and another Christianity that disagreed; and another Christianity that thought he died on the cross as a payment for sin and another Christianity that scoffed at that. This is nonsense."

"Still," I objected, "we do see the New Testament talking about controversies in the first century."

"Yes, and the New Testament quite honestly discusses disagreements when they occur—issues like circumcision, whether Christians can eat meat sacrificed to idols, those kind of tensions," he conceded. "But that's not what these scholars are claiming. They're trying to smuggle into the first century a mystical, Gnostic understanding of God and the Christian life, even though first century Christians had never heard of these things."

"So the core message of Christianity—"

"That Jesus is the Messiah, he's God's Son, he fulfills the scriptures, he died on the cross and thereby saved humanity, he rose from the dead—those core issues were not open for discussion, " he said.

Evans' mention of Gnosticism seemed an apt segue into discussing the most highly touted alternative text: the Gospel of Thomas.

DOCUMENT #1:
THE GOSPEL OF THOMAS

"History preserves at least half a dozen references that say there was a gospel purportedly written by Thomas," Evans said in response to my question about the document. "And, by the way, they didn't believe for a minute that this gospel really went back to the disciple Thomas or that it was authentic or early. Nobody was saying, 'Boy, I wish we could find that lost Gospel of Thomas because it's a goodie.' They were saying, 'Somebody cooked this up and it goes by the name of Thomas, but nobody believes that.'"

In 1945, a copy of the Gospel of Thomas in Coptic was discovered in Egypt among thirteen leather-bound codices preserved in a jar, Evans said.

"What's particularly interesting is that most of the material in Thomas parallels Matthew, Mark, Luke, John, and sometimes Paul and other sources. Over half of the New Testament writings are quoted, paralleled, or alluded to in Thomas."

"What does that tell you?" I asked.

"It tells me it's late," he replied. "I'm not aware of a Christian writing prior to 150 that references this much of the New Testament. Go to the Epistles of Ignatius, the bishop of Antioch, which were written around AD 110. They don't quote even half of the New Testament. Then along comes the Gospel of Thomas and it shows familiarity with fourteen or fifteen of the twenty-seven New Testament writings." His eyebrows shot up. "And people want to date it to the middle of the first century? Come on!"

I interrupted. "Elaine Pagels told me that she takes what she called a 'conservative view' of the dating and puts it at about AD 80 or 90. Stevan L. Davies says Thomas 'is wholly independent of the New Testament Gospels; most probably it was in existence before they were written. It should be dated AD 50–70.'"[12]

"Oh, that's absurd!"

Undeterred, I continued. "John Dominic Crossan says the current text emerged about 60 or 70, but that an earlier edition goes back as far as the 50s.[13] If they're right, that means Thomas has really early material. Are they wrong?"

"They're wrong for several reasons," he said. "Number one, as I explained, Thomas has too much New Testament in it. Not only that, but Thomas has forms that reflect the later developments in Luke or Matthew."

"Explain what you mean," I said.

"Matthew and Luke sometimes improve on Mark's grammar and word choice. Mark is not real polished in

terms of Greek grammar and style, while Matthew and
Luke are much more so. And in the Gospel of Thomas
we find these more polished Matthew and Luke forms
of the sayings of Jesus. So Thomas isn't referring to
the earlier Mark, but to the later Matthew and Luke.
We also find references to the special material that's
only found in Matthew and only in Luke, both of which
scholars think is later, not earlier.

"And Thomas has material from the Gospel of John.
How can Thomas be written in the 50s and the 60s but
still have Johannine material that doesn't get written
down until the 90s? It gets even worse when we find that
some of the material reflects *Syrian* development."

Again, I asked him to elaborate. "The Gospels are
published in the Greek language," he said. "Christianity then spread to all sorts of language groups. Of
course, it goes eastward, where people speak a form of
Aramaic called Syriac."

"So the Gospels were translated into Syriac?"

"Not immediately. There was a guy named Tatian
who created a written harmony of Matthew, Mark, Luke,
and John in the year 175. It's called the *Diatessaron*,
which means, 'through the four.' What he did was blend
all four Gospels together and present it in Syriac. So
the first time Syrian-speaking Christians had access to
the Gospels was not as separate Matthew, Mark, Luke,
and John, but as the blended, harmonized form.

"In blending together the sayings of the four Gospels, Tatian created some new forms, because it was
part Matthew, part Luke, and so forth. Here's the

clincher: those distinctive Syrian forms show up in the gospel of Thomas.

"What's more, a study by Nicholas Perrin has found that in places the Gospel of Thomas is also acquainted with the order and arrangement of material in the *Diatessaron*. All of this means Thomas must have been written *later* than the *Diatessaron* in 175. Now everything begins to add up. Of course Thomas knows more than half of the New Testament. By the end of the second century, you're in a position to know that much. And Thomas reflects Syrian ideas."

"Such as what?"

Evans replied with a question of his own: "How does the Gospel of Thomas refer to Thomas?"

"As Judas Thomas," I offered.

"That's right," he said. "That name is found in the Syrian church — and nowhere else. Also, the Syrian church was very much into ascetics. They did not like wealth. They did not like businessmen and commercialism. That shows up in Thomas. They were into elitism and mysticism. And guess what? That also shows up in Thomas.

"But maybe this is the most interesting evidence. If you read Thomas in Greek or Coptic, it looks like the 114 sayings [of Jesus] aren't in any particular order. But if you translate it into Syriac, something extremely intriguing emerges. Suddenly, you discover more than five hundred Syrian catchwords that link virtually all of the 114 sayings in order to help people memorize the gospel.[14] In other words, Saying 2 is followed by Saying 3 because Saying 2 refers to a certain word that's then contained in Saying 3. And Saying 3 has a certain word that leads you into Saying 4. It was a memorization aid.

"So you have distinctive Syrian sayings, you have Thomas called Judas Thomas, you have Syriac catchwords, you have familiarity with more than one-half of the New Testament—what does it all add up to? Everything points to Thomas being written at the end of the second century, no earlier than 175 and probably closer to 200."

I asked: "What about the argument that there's an earlier edition of Thomas, with more ancient elements, that's embedded in the text?"

"Obviously, Thomas is depending on some traditions that have been inherited. So, yes, there's some earlier stuff in it," he said. "But when you say there was an earlier Gospel of Thomas—a coherent, whole, discrete unit—now you're claiming something for which you should have evidence. Frankly, there is no such evidence."

"Do you think a legitimate argument can be made that Thomas should have been included in the Bible?" I asked.

"No, I'm sorry, it cannot," he insisted. "If Thomas is to be included, then why not the *Diatessaron*, because that's its source? Why not any mishmash written by anyone at the end of the second century that takes second- and third-hand materials, blends them together, and creates an inauthentic setting? Matthew,

Mark, Luke, and John were earlier than all of these other gospels, and they have credible connections with the first-generation, apostolic, eyewitness sources. The only way to deny that is to say, well, I don't care what the evidence says."

DOCUMENT #2:
THE GOSPEL OF MARY

Popularized by Dan Brown's novel *The Da Vinci Code*, the Gospel of Mary has become increasingly fashionable, especially among women who interpret it as validating female leadership in the church. "What about any historical connection with Mary herself?" I asked Evans.

"Nobody in all seriousness who's a scholar and is competent would say Mary Magdalene composed this gospel that now bears her name."

"Her name was attached to legitimize it?" I asked.

"Sure. That's what Gnostics would do. In contrast, the Gospels of Matthew, Mark, and Luke circulated anonymously. Everybody knew this was what Jesus taught, so there wasn't much concern over who wrote it down. But the gospels of the second century and later would attach a first-century name to try to bootstrap their credibility, since they didn't sound like Jesus."

"You'd date the Gospel of Mary to the second century?"

"Yes, probably between 150 and 200," he replied. "And, frankly, that's not very controversial. Scholars are virtually unanimous about this. There's nothing in it that we can trace back with any confidence to the first century, or to the historical Jesus, or to the historical Mary."

DOCUMENT #3:
THE GOSPEL OF JUDAS

In 2006, Evans was among the biblical scholars who unveiled the long-lost Gospel of Judas, which was discovered in the late 1970s and took a circuitous route to end up the focus of intense worldwide interest.

Carbon 14 tests dated the papyrus to AD 220 to 340, although many scholars lean toward 300 to 320. The original gospel, however, was written prior to 180, which is when the church father Irenaeus warned about this "fictitious history."[15]

Its most sensational claims are that Judas Iscariot was Jesus' greatest disciple, who alone was able to understand Jesus' most profound teaching, and that the two of them conspired to arrange for Jesus' betrayal. "You will exceed them all," Jesus is quoted as telling Judas, "for you will sacrifice the man who clothes me." If true, this would cast Judas and Jesus in a much different light than has traditionally been accepted.

"Is there anything historical about Jesus and Judas in this document?" I asked.

"Probably not," Evans said. "Notice, by the way, that the document calls itself the 'Gospel *of* Judas,' not the 'Gospel *According to* Judas,' as we have in the New

Testament Gospels. So whoever wrote this document may have been indicating that Judas should not be understood as the author of the gospel, but rather that this is a gospel *about* Judas. In any event, it's written long after Judas lived. But still, it does have historical significance."

"How so?"

"It tells us Irenaeus knew what he was talking about when he wrote that this gospel existed, so that's another point in favor of his credibility. It tells us something about second century Gnosticism and perhaps a group called the Cainites, who are a bit mysterious to us."

"What did they believe?"

"They identified with the villains of the Bible," he said. "They believed that the god of this world is evil, and so anyone that he hates must really be a hero. So they would lionize Cain, Esau, the people of Sodom — and naturally Judas fits right in there. Just how positive the portrait of Judas is in this new text remains an open question."

I said, "You and the other scholars have been careful to caution that this gospel doesn't really tell us anything reliable about Jesus or Judas. But I've seen all kinds of wild speculation. Does that concern you?"

"Unfortunately, it's a reflection of what we've seen with some of these other gospels," he replied. "Just because something's on a screen or in a book doesn't mean it's true. I'd caution people to apply the historical tests I mentioned earlier and then make a reasoned judgment instead of being influenced by irresponsible conspiracy theories and other historical nonsense."

Testing the Bible's Four Gospels

All of this brought me back to Matthew, Mark, Luke, and John. How do they fare when subjected to a historian's scrutiny? I asked Evans what he considered to be the best criteria for assessing their reliability.

"One criterion historians use is multiple attestation," he replied. "In other words, when two or three of the Gospels are saying the same thing, independently — as they often do — then this significantly shifts the burden of proof onto somebody who says they're just making it up. There's also the criterion of coherence. Are the Gospels consistent with what we know about the history and culture of Palestine in the 20s and 30s? Actually, they're loaded with details that we've determined are correct thanks to archaeological discoveries.

"Then there's the dating issue. The Synoptics [Matthew, Mark, and Luke] were written within a generation of Jesus' ministry; John is within two generations. That encourages us to see them as reliable because they're written too close to the events to get away with a bunch of lies. And you don't have any counter-gospels that are repudiating or refuting what they say.

"We have, then, a treasure trove from any historian's point of view. Julius Caesar died in 44 BC, and the historian Suetonius is talking about him in AD 110–20.

That's about 155 to 165 years removed. Tacitus, same thing. The Gospels are much better than that."

"When would you date them?"

"Very cogent arguments have been made for all three Synoptics having been written in the 50s and 60s. Personally, I'd put the first gospel, Mark, in the 60s. I think Mark had to have been within the shadow of the Jewish-Roman war of 66–70. Jesus says in Mark 13:18, 'Pray that this will not take place in winter.' Well, it didn't. It happened in the summer. This statement makes sense if Mark was published when the war was underway or about to occur. But if it was written in 71 or 72, as some have speculated, that would be an odd statement to leave in place."

I interrupted. "But whether Mark was written in the 50s or 60s, you're still talking very early."

"Absolutely. Jesus died in AD 30 or 33, and a lot of scholars lean toward 33. That means when Mark's Gospel was composed, some of Jesus' youngest followers and disciples would be in their 50s or 60s. Other people in their 30s and 40s grew up hearing stories about Jesus from first-hand eyewitnesses. There's a density of witness that's very significant. And, of course, don't forget that most of Paul's writings were composed prior to the Gospels."

"So your assessment of their reliability is—what?"

"I would say the Gospels are essentially reliable, and there are lots and lots of other scholars who agree. There's every reason to conclude that the Gospels have fairly and accurately reported the essential elements of Jesus' teachings, life, death, and resurrection.

"They're early enough, they're rooted into the right streams that go back to Jesus and the original people, there's continuity, there's proximity, there's verification of certain distinct points with archaeology and other documents, and then there's the inner logic. That's what pulls it all together."

In the end, it was hard to disagree. The distorted image of Jesus promoted by the Gnostics simply vanishes like a mirage when exposed to scrutiny, while once again the biblical picture of Jesus becomes even more certain when the facts are examined.

CHAPTER 2

PORTRAIT #2:
THE MISQUOTED JESUS

Is His Story in the Bible Hopelessly Riddled with Errors?

> Please help me. I have just read Bart Ehrman's book *Misquoting Jesus*. I was raised in the church and I'm now 26 years old. This book has devastated my faith.... *Is Ehrman correct?*[1]

This was among the pleas I received in the wake of the 2005 best-selling book by Ehrman, head of religious studies at the University of North Carolina at Chapel Hill. A self-described Christian-turned-agnostic, Ehrman is a "textual critic," a scholar who analyzes biblical manuscripts to determine what the original copies—long ago dissolved into dust—actually said.

Until the printing press was invented, scribes made handwritten copies of the New Testament. Errors were inevitable—in fact, Ehrman reported there are 200,000 to 400,000 "variants," or differences, between the handwritten manuscripts.[2]

"How does it help us to say that the Bible is the inerrant word of God if in fact we don't have the words that God inerrantly inspired, but only the words copied by the scribes—sometimes correctly but sometimes (many times!) incorrectly?" Ehrman wrote.[3]

In addition, readers were stunned when Ehrman dismissed the authenticity of the famous story of Jesus forgiving the adulterous woman, the last twelve verses of Mark that describe Jesus' post-resurrection appearances, and the Bible's clearest passage on the Trinity.

Can the Bible's portrait of Jesus be trusted, or is it too pockmarked with errors to be accurate? To find out, I flew to Dallas to interview another renowned textual critic, Daniel B. Wallace, a professor of New Testament studies at Dallas Theological Seminary and executive director of the Center for the Study of New Testament Manuscripts.

Wallace has done postdoctoral study at Tyndale House, Cambridge, as well as at Tübingen University and the *Institut für Neutestamentliche Textforschung*. He's the senior New Testament editor of the NET Bible and coauthor of several books, including *Reinventing Jesus*. Wallace is best known for his textbook *Greek Grammar Beyond the Basics*, which is used by most schools that teach intermediate Greek, including Yale, Princeton, and Cambridge.

Challenging Our Biases

I stopped by Wallace's house and we settled into chairs in his two-story library, which has a capacity of six thousand books. "One scholar wrote that Ehrman 'has a strong ax to grind,'"[4] I said. "But doesn't this cut both ways? Scholars who argue for the reliability of the New Testament might also be accused of bias."

"You can't interpret the text without certain biases, but we should challenge our biases as much as possible," Wallace replied. "One way to do that is to look for viewpoints that are shared by more than one group of people. The fact is that scholars across the theological spectrum say that in all essentials — not in every particular, but in *all* essentials — our New Testament manuscripts go back to the originals.

"Ehrman is part of a very small minority of textual critics in what he's saying. Frankly, I don't think he has challenged his biases; instead, I think he has fed them. Readers end up having far more doubts about what the Bible says than any textual critic today would ever have. I think Ehrman has simply overstated his case."

An Embarrassment of Riches

Scholars reconstructing the original text of the New Testament have thousands of manuscripts to work with. The more copies, the easier it is to discern the contents of the original. Given their centrality to textual criticism, I asked Wallace to talk about the quantity and quality of New Testament documents.

"Quite simply, we have more witnesses to the text of the New Testament than to any other ancient Greek or Latin literature. It's really an embarrassment of riches!" he declared.

"We have more than 5,700 Greek copies of the New

Testament. There are another 10,000 copies in Latin. Then there are versions in other languages — Coptic, Syriac, Armenian, Georgian, and so on. These are estimated to number between 10,000 and 15,000. So right there we've got 25,000 to 30,000 handwritten copies of the New Testament."

"But aren't many of these merely fragments?"

"A great majority of these manuscripts are complete for the purposes that the scribes intended. For example, some manuscripts were intended just to include the Gospels; others, just Paul's letters. Only sixty Greek manuscripts have the entire New Testament, but that doesn't mean that most manuscripts are fragmentary."

In addition, said Wallace, "The ancient church fathers quoted so often from the New Testament that it would be possible to reconstruct almost the entire New Testament from their writings alone. All told, there are more than one *million* quotations of the New Testament in their writings. They date as early as the first century and continue through the thirteenth century.

"The quantity and quality of the New Testament manuscripts are unequalled in the ancient Greco-Roman world. The average Greek author has fewer than twenty copies of his works still in existence, and they come from no sooner than five hundred to a thousand years later. If you stacked the copies of his works on top of each other, they would be about four feet tall. Stack up copies of the New Testament and they would reach more than a mile high — and, again, that doesn't include quotations from the church fathers."

I asked Wallace about the dates of the documents. "About ten percent of these manuscripts come from the first millennium," he said. "Through the first three centuries, we have nearly fifty manuscripts in Greek alone."

One famous fragment, he said, is a papyrus containing John 18:31–33 and 18:37–38. Discovered in 1934, it has been dated to between AD 110 and 150, with the earlier date preferred. One expert dates it to the 90s. This has devastated liberal claims that John wasn't written until 160 or 170.

"Is that the only fragment from the second century?" I asked.

"Not only isn't it the only one, but in the last five years at least three or four others have also been found from the second century in a museum at Oxford. They were excavated in 1906, and have been sitting there for nearly a century. To date we have between ten to fifteen papyri from the second century. It's absolutely stunning!

"And even though they're fragmentary, they're not always small. We have, for example, P^{66}, which is from mid-to-late second century and has almost the entirety of John's Gospel. P^{46}, which dates to about AD 200, has got seven of Paul's letters and Hebrews in it. P^{75}, which is late second century to early third century, has John and Luke almost in their entirety. P^{45} is early too—and it has large portions of the four Gospels, so that's a substantial amount of evidence."

"So we have a really small gap, then, between the

earliest papyrus and the New Testament documents," I said.

"Right. There's just no comparison to others," he said. "For other great historians, there's a three-hundred-year gap before you get a sliver of a fragment, and then sometimes you have to wait another thousand years before you see something else."

Explaining the Variants

Ehrman reported that there are 200,000 to 400,000 variants between New Testament manuscripts. This was old news to textual critics, but it shocked the public. Yet do these variants jeopardize the Bible's depiction of Jesus?

"If there's any manuscript or church father who has a different word in one place, that counts as a textual variant," Wallace explained. "If you have a thousand manuscripts that have, for instance, 'Lord' in John 4:1, and all the rest of the manuscripts have 'Jesus,' that still counts as only one variant. If a single fourteenth-century manuscript misspells a word, that counts as a variant.

"Far and away, the most common are spelling variations, even when the misspelling in Greek makes absolutely no difference in the meaning of the word," he said.

"For example, the most common textual variant involves what's called a 'moveable *nu*.' The Greek letter nu — or 'n' — is used at the end of a word when the next word starts with a vowel. It's like in English, where

you have an indefinite article—*an* apple or *a* book.
Whether a *nu* appears in these words or not has absolutely no effect on its meaning. Yet they still record all
those as textual variants.

"Another example is that when you see the name
John, it's either spelled with one or two n's. They have
to record that as a textual variant—but how it comes
out in English is 'John' every time. It doesn't make
any difference. Somewhere between seventy to eighty
percent of all textual variants are spelling differences
that can't even be translated into English and have zero
impact on meaning."

I did some mental math. Taking the high estimate of
400,000 variants, that would mean 280,000 to 320,000
would be inconsequential spelling differences.

"Then you've got nonsense errors, where a scribe
was inattentive and makes a mistake that's an obvious
no-brainer to spot," he said. "For example, in a manuscript in the Smithsonian Institution, one scribe wrote
the word 'and' when he meant to write 'Lord.' It was
obvious that the word 'and' doesn't fit the context. So in
these cases, it's easy to reconstruct the right word.

"There are also variants involving synonyms. Does
John 4:1 say, 'When Jesus knew' or 'When the Lord
knew'? We're not sure which goes back to the original,
but both words are true. A lot of variants involve the
Greek practice of using a definite article with a proper
name, which we don't do in English. For example, a
manuscript might refer to 'the Mary' but the scribe

might have simply written 'Mary.' Again, there's no impact on meaning, but they're counted as variants.

"On top of that, you've got variants that can't even be translated into English. Greek is a highly inflected language. That means the order of words in Greek isn't as important as it is in English. For example, there are sixteen different ways in Greek to say, 'Jesus loves Paul,' and they would be translated into English the very same way. Still, it counts as a textual variant if there's a difference in the order of words, even if the meaning is unaffected.

"So if we have approximately 200,000 to 400,000 variants, I'm just shocked that there are so few!" he declared. "What would the potential number be? Tens of *millions*! Part of the reason we have so many variants is because we have so many manuscripts. And we're glad we've got so many manuscripts — it helps us immensely in getting back to the original."

"How many textual variants really make a difference?" I asked.

"Only about one percent of variants are both meaningful, which means they affect the meaning of the text to some degree, and viable, which means they have a decent chance of going back to the original text. But most of these are not very significant at all," he said.

"I'll describe two of the most notorious issues. One involves Romans 5:1. Did Paul say, 'We *have* peace' or '*let us have* peace'? The difference amounts to one letter in the Greek. Scholars are split on this, but the big point is that neither variant is a contradiction of the teachings of scripture.

"Another famous example is First John 1:4. The verse says either, 'Thus we are writing these things so that *our* joy may be complete,' or, 'Thus we are writing these things so that *your* joy may be complete.' There's ancient testimony for both readings. So, yes, the meaning is affected, but no foundational beliefs are in jeopardy. Either way, the obvious meaning of the verse is that the writing of this letter brings joy."

Intentional Changes

Ehrman put a lot of emphasis on scribes who intentionally altered the text. "That makes people very nervous," I said.

"Well, he's absolutely correct," Wallace replied. "Sometimes scribes did intentionally change the text."

"What's the most common reason?" I asked.

"They wanted to make the text more explicit. For example, the church started using sections of scripture for daily readings. These are called lectionaries. They set forth a year's worth of daily or weekly scripture readings.

"In the Gospel of Mark, there are eighty-nine verses in a row where the name of Jesus isn't mentioned once. Just pronouns are used, with 'he' referring to Jesus. Well, if you excerpt a passage for a daily lectionary reading, you can't start with: 'When he was going someplace....' The reader wouldn't know whom you were referring to. So it was logical for the scribe to replace 'he' with 'Jesus' in order to be more specific in the lectionary. But it's counted as a variant every time.

"Now, I don't want to give the impression that the scribes didn't ever change the text for theological reasons. They did, and almost always such changes were in the direction of making the New Testament *look* more orthodox. Probably the most common group of such changes are harmonizations between the Gospels. The further we get from the original text, the more the copyists harmonized so as to rid the text of any apparent discrepancies. But such harmonizations are fairly easy to detect."

"How many Christian doctrines are jeopardized by textual variants?"

"Ehrman is making the best case he can in *Misquoting Jesus*," Wallace said. "The remarkable thing is that you go through his whole book and you say, 'Where did he actually prove anything?' Ehrman didn't prove that *any* doctrine is jeopardized. Let me repeat the basic thesis that has been argued since 1707: *No cardinal or essential doctrine is altered by any textual variant that has plausibility of going back to the original.* The evidence for that has not changed to this day."

"What comes the closest?"

"Mark 9:29 could impact orthopraxy, which is right practice, but not orthodoxy, which is right belief. Here Jesus says you can't cast out a certain kind of demon except by prayer — and some manuscripts add, 'and fasting.' So if 'and fasting' is part of what Jesus said, then here's a textual variant that affects orthopraxy—is it necessary to fast to do certain kinds of exorcisms?

"But, seriously, does my salvation depend on that?" he said. "Most Christians have never even heard of that verse or will ever perform an exorcism."

Endearing, but Inauthentic

It's one of the most beloved Bible stories: a woman caught in adultery is brought before Jesus by the Pharisees. But instead of saying she should be stoned to death, Jesus uttered those often-quoted words, "If any one of you is without sin, let him be the first to throw a stone at her." Chastened, the Pharisees departed. Jesus then dismissed the woman by saying, "Go now and leave your life of sin."[5]

The problem: scholars have known for more than a century that this story is not authentic. This was disturbing news, though, to Ehrman's readers.

"When you read this passage, you say, 'Oh my gosh, that takes my breath away!'" Wallace said. "We say, 'I *want* this to be in the Bible.' And that's exactly what the copyists said. They read this as an independent story and ended up putting it in at least half a dozen different locations in John and Luke. It's as if the scribes said, 'I want this to go into my Bible, so I'm going to insert it here or here or here.'"

"So this was a story that came down through time?" I asked.

"Apparently, there were two different stories circulating about a woman who had been caught in some sin and Jesus was merciful to her. More than likely, that much of the story was historically true, but it didn't end up in the scriptures.

"My hypothesis is this: these verses look more like Luke's style and vocabulary than John's. Actually, a group of manuscripts put it in Luke instead of John. What did the story look like when Luke had access to it, and why didn't he put it into his Gospel? I don't have the answers yet."

"But it's clear that the story in the Bible is not authentic," I said.

"Is it *literarily* authentic—in other words, did John write this story? My answer is an unquestionable no. Is it *historically* authentic? Did it really happen? My answer is a highly qualified yes—something may have happened with Jesus being merciful to a sinner, but the story was originally in a truncated form.

"Read any Bible translation and you'll find a marginal note that says this is not found in the oldest manuscripts. But often people don't read those. When Ehrman reports in the popular sphere that the story isn't authentic, people think they've been hoodwinked."

Snakes and Tongues

In 2006, a woman died after being bitten by a rattlesnake during Sunday services at a Kentucky church.[6] Journalists reporting the death said that according to the Gospel of Mark, Christians should be able to handle snakes without harm. However, none of them noted that this verse—in fact, the last twelve verses of

Mark — were not part of the original Gospel, but were added later and are not authentic.

This means Mark ends with three women discovering the empty tomb of Jesus and being told by "a young man dressed in a white robe" that Jesus had risen from the dead. "They said nothing to anyone," concludes the Gospel, "because they were afraid." The final twelve verses describe three post-Easter appearances by Jesus and say Christians will be able to safely handle snakes, cast out demons, speak in new tongues, and heal the sick.

But Wallace explained that *Codex Vaticanus* and *Codex Sinaiticus* are "our oldest manuscripts for this passage" and neither of them has these twelve verses.

"Where do you think this ending came from?" I asked.

"There are two basic views. One group says Mark wrote an ending to his Gospel but it was lost."

He sounded skeptical. "You don't buy that?"

"This presupposes that Mark was written on a codex rather than a scroll. A page could be lost fairly easily from a codex, because the binding is like a book, but the ending of the Gospel would have been secure on a scroll. However, the codex wasn't invented until forty or so years after Mark was written.

"I think a far better view is that Mark was writing about the most unique individual who has ever lived, and he wanted to format the ending of his Gospel in a unique way, in which he leaves it open-ended. He's essentially saying to readers, 'So what are *you* going to do with Jesus?'"

"Eliminating those twelve verses, then, has no impact on the doctrine of the resurrection?"

"Not in the slightest. There's still a resurrection in Mark. It's prophesied, the angel attests to it, and the tomb is empty. I think a scribe in the second century drew essentially on Acts—where Paul gets bitten by a snake and people are speaking in tongues—and he wanted to round out Mark's Gospel so he put on that new ending.

"All Bibles have a note indicating this longer ending isn't in the oldest manuscripts. Some put these verses in smaller type or otherwise bracket it. Of the disputed verses in the Bible, this and the woman caught in adultery are by far the longest passages—and again, they're old news."

However, Ehrman also discussed "the only passage in the entire Bible that explicitly delineates the doctrine of the Trinity," which is found in First John 5:7–8—only in the King James Version. It says: "For there are three that bear record in heaven, the Father, the Word, and the Holy Ghost: and these three are one."

"Wouldn't you agree this is inauthentic?" I asked.

"Absolutely. That actually came from a homily in the eighth century. It was added to a Latin text and wasn't even translated into Greek until 1520. It's obviously inauthentic."

"Atheist Frank Zindler says that deleting this

reference 'leaves Christians without biblical proof of the Trinity,'" I observed.[7]

"I'm going to be uncharitable here: that's just such a stupid comment, I can hardly believe it," he said. "The Council of Constantinople in AD 381 and Chalcedon in AD 451 emerged with explicit statements affirming the Trinity — obviously, they didn't need this later, inauthentic passage to see it.

"The Bible clearly contains these four truths: the Father is God, Jesus is God, the Holy Spirit is God, and there's only one God," Wallace said. "And *that's* the Trinity."

Doctor-Father

My interview with Wallace strongly affirmed my confidence in the New Testament text. Nothing produced by Ehrman even came close to changing the traditional portrait of the real Jesus in any meaningful way.

As I drove away from Wallace's house, my mind flashed back to my interview several years earlier with a scholar who was considered the greatest textual critic of his generation. In fact, Bruce M. Metzger was Ehrman's mentor at Princeton. Ehrman even dedicates *Misquoting Jesus* to him.[8]

I remember asking Metzger, "So the variations [between manuscripts], when they occur, tend to be minor rather than substantive?"

"Yes, yes, that's correct," Metzger replied. "The

more significant variations do not overthrow any doctrine of the church."

Then I recall asking him how his many decades of intensely studying the New Testament text had affected his personal faith. "Oh," he said, "it has increased the basis of my personal faith to see the firmness with which these materials have come down to us, with a multiplicity of copies, some of which are very ancient."

"So scholarship has not diluted your faith—"

He jumped in. "On the contrary," he stressed, "it has built it. I've asked questions all my life, I've dug into the text, I've studied this thoroughly, and today I know with confidence that my trust in Jesus has been well placed. "

Then he added for emphasis, "*Very* well placed."[9]

CHAPTER 3

PORTRAIT #3:
THE FAILED JESUS

Was He Unsuccessful in Fulfilling
the Ancient Prophecies?

Jewish and Christian scholars agree: the Hebrew scriptures foretell the coming of the Messiah. "Belief in the coming of the Messiah has always been a fundamental part of Judaism," said Rabbi Aryeh Kaplan. "It is a concept that is repeated again and again throughout the length and breadth of Jewish literature."[1]

The big controversy is whether Jesus fulfilled the ancient messianic prophecies and thus matches the portrait of the Messiah, a word meaning "anointed one." The Greek word for Messiah is *christos*, or Christ, the term customarily affixed to Jesus' name.

If these messianic predictions really did come true in Jesus, the implications are enormous. First, this would confirm the supernatural nature of the Bible, since the odds of fulfilling so many ancient prophecies by mere chance would be mathematically prohibitive. Second, if only Jesus fulfilled these ancient prophecies, then this would be a definitive affirmation of his identity as the one sent by God to be the Savior of Israel and the world.

Of course, the opposite is also true. When a Samaritan woman said to Jesus, "I know that Messiah is coming," he replied: "I who speak to you am he."[2] Having made this unambiguous claim, if Jesus then failed to match the prophetic portrait, he would be an imposter worthy of rejection and disdain—a false prophet who should be rejected by Jews and Gentiles alike.

Historically, Jewish rabbis have rejected Jesus' messianic credentials. They point out that he didn't fulfill what they consider to be the main messianic prophecies: bringing about a world of peace and unity, and ending evil, idolatry, falsehood, and hatred. "The Jews had one major objection to the Christian Messiah," said Kaplan, "and that was the fact that he had been unsuccessful."[3]

Said Amy-Jill Levine, a Jewish expert in the New Testament: "The Messiah is someone who establishes justice throughout the world, and I look out my window and I know that hasn't happened."[4]

Christians offer a different perspective. "Not all of the prophecies in the Old Testament about the Messiah were fulfilled in Jesus' lifetime," said ancient-history professor Edwin Yamauchi. "The Christians' answer is that those prophecies will be fulfilled when Christ comes again."[5]

One thing is for sure: history and logic either support the conclusion that Jesus is the Messiah or they don't. To investigate the case for Jesus being the Messiah,

I flew to Charlotte to interview Michael L. Brown, a scholar who grew up Jewish and became convinced that Jesus really is the Messiah.

With a doctorate in Near Eastern Languages and Literatures from New York University, Brown has taught at Trinity Evangelical Divinity School, Fuller Theological Seminary, and in twenty-five countries. He has authored eighteen books, including the multi-volume *Answering Jewish Objections to Jesus*, which responds to historical and theological issues regarding the messianic prophecies.

I sat with Brown in his office at a school of ministry where he serves as president, the twenty volumes of the Babylonian Talmud on a sagging shelf over his shoulder, and asked him to set forth the evidence for Jesus being the Messiah.

The Case for Jesus the Messiah

"The Jews are God's chosen people," he began. "But it's important to understand that when God chose Abraham and his descendants, there was a divine purpose. It was not just to have a separated people who would be loyal to him; it was so that through Israel the entire world would be blessed and come to know the one true God. We need to keep that in mind as we proceed."

I nodded in acknowledgement.

"There are specific promises given to the tribe of Judah and to David, who was from the tribe of Judah and was the son of Jesse," Brown continued. "Genesis

49:10 says, 'The scepter will not depart from Judah,' while Isaiah 11:1 says, 'A shoot will come up from the stump of Jesse; from his roots a Branch will bear fruit.' The term 'Branch' is commonly used to refer to the Messiah. It's said there would be a lasting kingship through David. The Lord declares in Jeremiah 23:5 that he will raise up from David's line 'a righteous Branch, a King who will reign wisely.'"

So far, nothing controversial.

"When we get to Isaiah, we see references to the servant of the Lord. A number of these verses are also recognized as referring to the Messiah in some ancient Jewish traditions. Isaiah 42 says he will not falter until he brings justice to the earth.[6] Isaiah 49 says the servant has the mission of regathering the tribes of Israel to bring them back to God. The servant feels as if he failed in his mission, but God says not only will he ultimately regather Israel, but he adds in Isaiah 49:6, 'I will also make you a light for the Gentiles, that you may bring salvation to the ends of the earth.'"

Then Brown brought up the most famous messianic passage of all—Isaiah 52:13 to 53:12. "These verses say the Messiah will be highly exalted but first will suffer terribly. He will actually be disfigured in his suffering," Brown explained. "And the narrative says the people of Israel didn't get it. They thought he was suffering for his own sins and wickedness; they didn't realize he was bearing *their* sins, suffering on *their* behalf, and by his wounds there was healing for them.

Then it speaks of his death and his continued life after that.

"Now we narrow things even more. In Second Chronicles 7, God says if Israel's sin reaches a certain level, he'll destroy the temple, exile the people, and leave them in a state of judgment.[7] Sure enough, this comes to pass. The prophet Daniel prays in Daniel 9 that God would have mercy. God gives him a revelation about the temple being rebuilt. Before this new temple is destroyed, Daniel is told, several things are going to take place, including the bringing of everlasting atonement—the final dealing with sin.[8]

"The prophet Haggai lives to see this second temple built, but it's nothing like the first. The first one, Solomon's temple, was not only a stunning physical structure far more imposing than the second temple, but it had the glory of God there. When sacrifices were offered, fire came down and consumed them. The second temple didn't have the presence of God or the divine fire.

"Yet Haggai said the glory of the second temple would be greater than the glory of the first temple. God would fill the second temple with his glory.[9] The Hebrew word for glory can sometimes refer to great wealth and abundance, but when God says he'll *fill* the Temple with *glory*, that can only apply to his presence. Then the prophet Malachi, who lived later, says the Lord will come to his temple, purifying some of his people and bringing judgment on others.[10] He uses a Hebrew term that always refers to God himself: *the* Lord—*he* will come to that temple.

"Keep in mind the second temple was destroyed in AD 70. Atonement for sin had to be made and the divine visitation had to take place before the second temple was destroyed. There are even rabbinic traditions that put the Messiah's coming around two thousand years ago—right when Jesus came.[11]

"So it's not a matter of maybe there's another one who's the Messiah. If it's not Yeshua, which is the Jewish name for Jesus, then throw out the Bible, because nobody except him accomplished what needed to be done prior to AD 70. What divine visitation *did* take place if not for Yeshua? When else *did* God visit the second temple in a personal way? Who else atoned for sin? How else *was* the glory of the second temple greater than the first? Either the Messiah came two thousand years ago or the prophets were wrong and we can discard the Bible. But they weren't wrong. Yeshua is the Messiah—or nobody is."

He paused to let the implications sink in. "Let's keep going," Brown continued. "The Talmud asks whether the Messiah will come 'with the clouds of heaven,' as written in Daniel 7:13, or 'lowly and riding upon a donkey,' as in Zechariah 9:9.[12] The rabbis said if we're worthy, he'll come with the clouds of heaven, meaning swiftly and powerfully; if we're unworthy, he'll come meek and lowly. They believed it's 'either/or.' Actually, it's 'both/and.' They're both true—of the same person.

"Shortly before he died, Jesus rode on a donkey into Jerusalem, with the crowds hailing him as the Messiah. But then the people turned on him. Is it possible that he came 'lowly and riding upon a donkey' because we weren't worthy of his coming, and in the future, when we recognize him as the Messiah, he will return with the clouds of heaven, as he himself specifically foretold in his trial before the high priest?"

Brown moved ahead without waiting for an answer. "Now let's think about the roles of the Messiah," he continued. "In addition to being a king, he would be a priestly figure."

"How do you know?" I interrupted.

"Well, David is the prototype for the Messiah, and David performed certain priestly functions," Brown said. "Second Samuel 24:25 says, 'David built an altar to the LORD there and sacrificed burnt offerings and fellowship offerings.' That's what a priest does. According to Second Samuel 8:18, David's sons were priests.

"Then look at Psalm 110:4. It says, 'The LORD has sworn and will not change his mind: you are a priest forever in the order of Melchizedek.' Here we have the Lord making an emphatic oath that the king in Jerusalem was to be a priest forever in the order of the ancient priest-king of that city. Either this prophecy directly refers to the Messiah or it refers to David. If it refers to David, and he's the prototype of the Messiah, it still means the Messiah will be priestly as well as royal.

"In Zechariah 3, we encounter Jeshua, who was the high priest. Incidentally, Jeshua is the short form of the name Joshua, which in English would be Jesus. Jeshua is said to be a sign and symbol of 'the Branch.' Remember, Jeremiah 23 and other passages tell us the Branch is the Messiah, because he's the branch that comes out from the tree, the root of Jesse. In Zechariah 6:11–13, Jeshua is sitting on a throne. They put a crown on his head. So think about this: in the most overt passage in the Bible where a human being is explicitly identified with a Messianic figure, it's a high priest sitting on a throne."

Brown paused for emphasis. "A *priestly* king!" he stressed. "Typically, priests don't sit on thrones and priests don't have crowns."

"Why is this important?" I asked.

"Because priests dealt with sin. Priests bore the iniquities of the people on their shoulders. They were intercessors. In fact, according to Numbers 35, the death of the high priest could serve as atonement for certain sins for which there were no other earthly atonement.

"Now consider Psalm 22. This isn't a prophecy; it's a prayer of a righteous sufferer who comes to the jaws of death and is miraculously delivered. Yet Jesus said that everything written up to his lifetime finds its full meaning and expression in him. He even applied Psalm 22 to himself on the cross.[13] And in Psalm 22, as a result of the righteous sufferer's deliverance from death, all the ends of the earth will worship God.[14] That's quite a significant deliverance from death!

"So let's put all of this together. God's intent was not to keep Israel as an isolated nation, but that through

Israel the entire world will come to know the one true God. That has always been his heart. We see in the scriptures that this messianic figure will be both priestly *and* royal — he will deal with sin as well as rule and reign. He will first suffer before he is raised up and exalted; he will come riding on a donkey meek and lowly, as well as come in clouds of glory.

"He will first be rejected by his people and will be a light to the nations. He will suffer terribly for our sins as a righteous substitute. The power of his deliverance from death will cause the ends of the earth to worship the one true God. We also see that redemption had to come and there had to be divine visitation before the second temple was destroyed in AD 70."

Brown reached his hands toward me as if soliciting a response. "Who might that be?" he asked. "Is there any possible candidate? It's not rocket science to say either the Bible is false — or it has to be Yeshua."

"It's Him or No One"

Brown wasn't finished. "Yeshua said he came to fulfill what had been written in the Law and the Prophets. He predicted the destruction of the second temple. No other significant Jewish leader did that," he continued. "Deuteronomy 18 says to pay attention to the prophet who's raised up in each generation.[15] Yeshua is the last great prophet who speaks to Israel. He brings this prophetic word: The temple is going to be destroyed, but the fulfillment of what's written in the scriptures points to him.

"In short, Yeshua fulfilled the essential prophecies that had a definite time frame and which had to be completed before the second temple was destroyed. This is not a matter of speculation; it's historical fact. And since he fulfilled the past prophecies — coming as our great high priest and making atonement for our sins — we can be sure that he will fulfill the future prophecies, reigning as the worldwide king and bringing peace to the earth.

"In fact, he already rules and reigns as a royal king over the lives of countless tens of millions of people from every nation under the sun. They give him their total allegiance and loyalty. His reign is already far greater and more influential than the reign of David himself. And that's only the beginning; he will reign over all when he returns.

"Think about this: For more than 1,900 years, traditional Jews have had no functioning temple. There has been no functioning priesthood with sacrifices. What happened? As you read through the Torah, or the first five books of the Bible, you find repeated references to sacrifices and offerings.[16] Isn't it significant that Isaiah 53 says the servant of the Lord will himself be a guilt offering?[17]

"Either God has left us completely bereft of the major atonement system, a functioning priesthood, and a functioning temple, or else everything that we're speaking of finds its fulfillment in the One who came when he had to come.

"We're not talking about things Yeshua could have

arranged. How do you arrange being the most influential Jew who ever lived? How do you arrange bringing hundreds of millions of people into the worship of God? How do you arrange being rejected by your people and yet being accepted by the nations? How do you arrange being the only possible candidate who can fulfill the scriptures, prophesying the end of one system and then bringing the reality of the new system?

"And here's something fascinating: There's a rabbinic tradition preserved in the Talmud that says on the Day of Atonement there were three different signs that the animal sacrifices the high priest offered had been accepted by God and atonement given to the nation.[18] In the years when the signs would come up negative, the people would be ashamed and mourn, because God had not accepted their sacrifice.

"Then it says that during the last forty years before the second temple was destroyed, all three signs were negative each and every time.[19] Think about that: Jesus was probably crucified in AD 30, and the temple was destroyed in AD 70. So from the time of his death to the time of the destruction of the temple — *a period of forty years* — God signaled that he no longer accepted the sacrifices and offerings of the Jewish people. Why?"

His answer was emphatic: *"Because final atonement had been made through Yeshua, just as he had prophesied."*

Brown let his words linger. Then, apparently sensing the need for elaboration, he said, "Please, let me explain how Yeshua fulfilled the Jewish sacrificial system."

"Yes, go ahead," I said.

"If you go through the first five books of the Bible, called the Written Torah, you'll find several hundred references to animal sacrifices and offerings," Brown said. "The fundamental concept was life for life, as recognized in some of the rabbinic commentaries. Why was it so important? Obviously, God was seeking to get something across—that sin required a penalty of death, and that God would receive a substitution on behalf of the guilty person. When an innocent lamb was slain and the blood drained out, that was quite a vivid lesson.

"Remember, it was foretold that the Messiah would be a priestly figure. What did the priest do? He went between the people and God. He went into the holiest place of all. By his stature, position, and calling, he did what nobody else could do. Yeshua, as the great high priest, prays for us and then literally carries our sins on his shoulders as Peter expresses—'He himself bore our sins in his body on the tree.'[20] He takes the guilt, the punishment, and the suffering that we all deserve, and bears them himself.

"What sacrifice is great enough to cover the guilt of the entire world? Who's pure enough? Who's perfect enough? Only this one, the great Son of God, takes the sin and guilt of the entire world on his own shoulders and dies on behalf of our sins so we can now receive forgiveness, cleansing, and righteousness. As we know from John 1:29, Yeshua was called 'the Lamb of God, who takes away the sin of the world.'"

Brown had been sitting on the edge of his chair. Now, his presentation complete, he eased back.

"So add everything up," he said. "All of these clues point to Yeshua and Yeshua alone. He fulfills the prophecies in the most incredible way. Since the Messiah had to come almost two thousand years ago, according to the testimony of the Jewish scriptures, then if Yeshua isn't the Messiah, there will never be a Messiah. It's too late for anyone else. If Yeshua didn't come and do what had to be done in the first phase of things, when there was a definite deadline, then there's no hope that the second phase will ever come, when he will come in the clouds of glory to rule and reign."

He smiled. "We have the deposit," he said. "We have the down payment. We can be confident he will return to accomplish the remainder."

However, I pointed out to Brown that the term *second coming* isn't found in the Hebrew scriptures.

"The word *trinity* isn't used anywhere in the entire Bible either, but the evidence is there supporting it," he countered. "The prophecies require certain events to happen—like atonement and the visit to the temple—before other events can happen, like the Messiah bringing peace to the earth. The first act precedes the second act and prepares the way for it. First atonement for sin, then peace on the earth."

"Couldn't the idea of a second coming be used

by any false Messiah who failed to fulfill all the prophecies?"

"Well, if Yeshua had done nothing to fulfill any of the prophecies and said he was going to do everything in the future, then, yes, I'd agree. But that's not the case," Brown said. "He did what needed to be done before AD 70, so we can have confidence he'll do what needs to be done in the future."

As Brown had powerfully established, Jesus—and no other figure throughout history—has matched the portrait of the Messiah. It's him—or it's nobody.

"That's why I'm spending my life talking to Jewish people—as compassionately and accurately as I can—about the reality of Jesus the Messiah," Brown concluded. "I just can't withhold God's very best from those he dearly loves."

CHAPTER 4

PORTRAIT #4:
THE UNCRUCIFIED JESUS

Did He Ever Really Die
on the Cross?

Iranian filmmaker Nader Talebzadeh is a fan of Mel
Gibson's 2004 blockbuster *The Passion of the Christ*.
The movie, he said, is superbly crafted. There is only
one problem: "The story," he insists, "is wrong."

So Talebzadeh produced his own documentary to
set the record straight. In *Jesus, the Spirit of God*, it's
Judas who is actually crucified after God rescues Jesus
at the last moment and takes him directly to heaven.
And since Jesus was never put to death, he was never
resurrected.[1]

Christians consider the resurrection of Jesus to be
a pivotal doctrine, since they believe it confirms his
identity as the unique Son of God. But Muslims like
Talebzadeh, who consider Jesus to be a mortal prophet,
are at the forefront of the most recent challenges to
the resurrection. They base their beliefs on the Qur'an,
which says that Jesus never died on the cross, much
less returned from the dead.[2]

A leading Muslim apologist, Shabir Ally, said the

Messiah was expected to be victorious, and therefore "a crucified Messiah is as self-refuting as a square circle."[3] In a 2006 videotape, Ayman al-Zawahri, the deputy leader of Al Qaeda, urged all Christians to convert to Islam, which, he said, correctly believes that Jesus was never put to death, never rose from the dead, and was not divine.[4]

Muslims aren't alone. A Hindu leader in India declared in 2007 that Jesus never died on the cross. "He was only injured and after treatment returned to India where he actually died," insisted K. S. Sudarshan.[5]

Another claim that Jesus wasn't killed by crucifixion came in the 2006 *New York Times* best-seller *The Jesus Papers*, in which Michael Baigent said Pontius Pilate didn't want to kill Jesus because Jesus had been urging people to pay their taxes.[6] That's when Pilate hatched a plot, Baigent said. He ordered Jesus crucified to placate the religious authorities who wanted him dead, but he conspired to ensure that Jesus secretly came down from the cross alive.[7]

Critics know that discrediting the resurrection means nothing less than disproving the truth of Christianity. "If Christ has not been raised," said the apostle Paul, "your faith is futile."[8] The cross either unmasked Jesus as a pretender or opened the door to a supernatural resurrection that has irrevocably confirmed his divinity. But where does the evidence point?

I invited prominent resurrection expert Michael Licona to my home to discuss these issues. Licona's dissertation toward his doctorate in New Testament from the University of Pretoria in South Africa uses historical methodologies to assess the evidence for Jesus returning from the dead.

Licona has debated numerous skeptics, including Muslims, about the resurrection and written extensively on the topic. In 2004, he joined resurrection scholar Gary Habermas in writing the award-winning book *The Case for the Resurrection of Jesus*. Using his impressive knowledge of Islam, Licona later authored *Paul Meets Muhammad: a Christian-Muslim Debate on the Resurrection*.

The Affirmative Evidence

As we sat in my family room, Licona set forth the affirmative case for Jesus being executed by the Romans.

"Even an extreme liberal like [John Dominic] Crossan says: 'That he was crucified is as sure as anything historical ever can be.'[9] Skeptic James Tabor says, 'I think we need have no doubt that given Jesus' execution by Roman crucifixion he was truly *dead*.'[10] Both Gerd Lüdemann, who's an atheistic New Testament critic, and Bart Ehrman, who's an agnostic, call the crucifixion an indisputable fact.

"Why? First of all, because all four Gospels report it. We also have a number of non-Christian sources that corroborate the crucifixion. For instance, the historian Tacitus said Jesus 'suffered the extreme penalty during the reign of Tiberius.' The Jewish historian Josephus reports that Pilate 'condemned him to be crucified.'

Lucian of Samosata, who was a Greek satirist, mentions the crucifixion, and Mara Bar-Serapion, who was a pagan, confirms Jesus was executed. Even the Jewish Talmud reports that 'Yeshu was hanged.'"

"Yeshu? Hanged?"

"Yes, Yeshu is Joshua in Hebrew; the Greek equivalent is translated as Jesus. And in the ancient world to be hung on a tree many times referred to a crucifixion. Galatians 3:13, for example, connects Jesus' crucifixion with the Pentateuch, which says that 'anyone who is hung on a tree is under God's curse.'"[11]

"What were the odds of surviving crucifixion?"

"Extremely small. You saw *The Passion of the Christ*, right? Even though not all of the film was historically accurate, it did depict the extreme brutality of Roman scourging and crucifixion. Witnesses in the ancient world reported victims being so severely whipped that their intestines and veins were laid bare."

"Did anyone ever survive it?"

"Josephus does mention three friends who were crucified. He doesn't say how long they had been on the cross, but he intervened with the Roman commander, who ordered all three removed immediately and provided the best medical attention Rome had to offer. Still, two died. So even under the best of conditions, a victim was unlikely to survive crucifixion. There is no evidence at all that Jesus was removed prematurely or that he was provided any medical attention whatsoever."

"We're dealing with a pretty primitive culture," I

observed. "Were they competent enough to be sure that Jesus was dead?"

"I'm confident they were. You've got Roman soldiers carrying out executions all the time. They were very good at it. Besides, death by crucifixion was basically a slow demise by asphyxiation, because of the difficulty in breathing created by the victim's position on the cross. And that's something you can't fake.

"Lee, Jesus was crucified and died as a result. The scholarly consensus — again, even among those who are skeptical toward the resurrection — is absolutely overwhelming. To deny it would be to take a marginal position that would get you laughed out of the academic world."

The Qur'an versus the Bible

I picked up my copy of the Qur'an. "You say Jesus was killed by crucifixion, but Muslims believe Jesus never really died on the cross," I said to Licona. Finding the fourth surah, I read aloud verses 157–158:

> That they said (in boast) "We killed Christ Jesus the son of Mary, the Messenger of Allah"; — but they did not kill him, nor crucified him, but so it was made to appear to them, and those who differ therein are full of doubts, with no (certain) knowledge, but only conjecture to follow, for of a surety they did not kill him; — Nay, Allah raised him up unto Himself; and Allah is Exalted in Power, Wise; — [12]

I closed the book. "There seem to be two possibilities: either someone was made to look like Jesus and the Romans killed that person, or Jesus was on the cross but Allah made it appear he died when he really didn't. They put him in a tomb, Allah healed him, and he was taken to heaven. Aren't those possible scenarios?"

"Well, anything is possible with God," Licona said, "but the real question is where does the evidence point? The question does not concern what God *can do*, but what God *did*. And the Qur'an is not a very credible source when it comes to Jesus."

"You don't believe the Qur'an has good credentials?"

"The Qur'an provides a test for people to verify its divine origin: gather the wisest people in the world and call upon the *jinn*, which are similar to demons but without necessarily all of the negative connotations, and try to write a surah, or chapter, that's as good as one in the Qur'an. The implication, of course, is that this can't be done."

"Do you think it can be?"

"I think so, rather easily. One person who speaks Arabic wrote what he calls *The True Furqan*, in which he maintains the style of the Qur'an in Arabic but with a message that's more Christian than Islamic.[13] Some Muslims heard portions of it read and were convinced that it was the Qur'an! So I guess the test has been passed. For those of us who can't read Arabic, we can perform a test by comparing the first surah of the Qur'an to Psalm 19 of the Bible."

Licona picked up my Qur'an to read the first surah out loud:

In the name of Allah, Most Gracious, Most Merciful.
Praise be to Allah, the Cherisher and Sustainer
    of the Worlds;
Most Gracious, Most Merciful;
Master of the Day of Judgment.
You do we worship, and Your aid do we seek.
Show us the straight way.
The way of those on whom You have bestowed
    Your Grace, those whose (portion) is not wrath,
    and who do not go astray.[14]

Closing the Qur'an, he then used his lap-top computer to access Psalm 19 and read it:

The heavens declare the glory of God;
    the skies proclaim the work of his hands.
Day after day they pour forth speech;
    night after night they display knowledge.
There is no speech or language
    where their voice is not heard.
Their voice goes out into all the earth,
    their words to the ends of the world.

In the heavens he has pitched a tent for the sun,
    which is like a bridegroom coming forth from his
        pavilion,
    like a champion rejoicing to run his course.
It rises at one end of the heavens
    and makes its circuit to the other;
    nothing is hidden from its heat.

*The law of the L*ORD *is perfect,*
      reviving the soul.
*The statutes of the L*ORD *are trustworthy,*
      making wise the simple.
*The precepts of the L*ORD *are right,*
      giving joy to the heart.
*The commands of the L*ORD *are radiant,*
      giving light to the eyes.
*The fear of the L*ORD *is pure,*
      enduring forever.
*The ordinances of the L*ORD *are sure*
      and altogether righteous.
They are more precious than gold,
      than much pure gold;
they are sweeter than honey,
      than honey from the comb.
By them is your servant warned;
      in keeping them there is great reward.

Who can discern his errors?
      Forgive my hidden faults.
Keep your servant also from willful sins;
      may they not rule over me.
Then will I be blameless,
      Innocent of great transgression.

May the words of my mouth and the meditation
            of my heart
      be pleasing in your sight,
      *O L*ORD, *my Rock and my Redeemer.*

"Both the surah and the psalm talk about the goodness and holiness of God," Licona said. "The psalm seems much more pregnant with meaning and much more beautiful to me. Granted, the Arabic surah has a poetic rhythm; however, so does the Hebrew psalm, which is actually a song."

"But Muslims would say you've got to read the surah in Arabic because it's got a beautiful flow in that language," I pointed out.

"I'd reply, 'Can you read Hebrew?'" said Licona. "If not, how do you know that the Arabic is better than the Hebrew song, which has a flowing rhythm similar to the surah? It really comes down to what language sounds best to you. It's very subjective. That's why it's not a good test of the Qur'an's divine nature.

"In contrast, Jesus provided a historical event — his resurrection — as the test by which we can know his message is true. Now, *that's* a good test, because a resurrection isn't going to happen unless God does it."

The Credibility of the Qur'an

I agreed with Licona — the supposed lyrical quality of the Qur'an was unavoidably a subjective test. "That's why you don't believe the Qur'an is credible?" I asked.

"That's only the beginning of the Qur'an's problems when it comes to Jesus," Licona said. "In addition, the Qur'an is fifth-hand testimony at best — the original Qur'an in heaven allegedly coming to us through an angel, then Muhammad, then those who recorded what Muhammad told them, then what was selected by Uthman. On top of that, you've got the Islamic Catch–22."

"The what?"

"Let me explain," he replied. "We can establish historically that Jesus predicted his own imminent and violent death. We find this reported in Mark, which is the earliest Gospel, and its multiplicity attested in different literary forms, which is really strong evidence in the eyes of historians.

"Also, consider the criterion of embarrassment. A lot of times when Jesus predicts his death, the disciples say, no, this can't happen, or they don't understand. This makes them look like knuckleheads, so it's embarrassing to the disciples to put this in the Gospel. This indicates that this is authentic, because you wouldn't make up something that puts the apostles in a bad light. Consequently, there are good historical reasons for believing Jesus did predict his imminent and violent demise."

"Okay, but where does the Islamic Catch–22 come in?"

"If Jesus did *not* die a violent and imminent death, then that makes him a false prophet. But the Qur'an says that he's a great prophet, and so the Qur'an would be wrong and thus discredited. On the other hand, if Jesus *did* die a violent and imminent death as he predicted, then he is indeed a great prophet — but this would contradict the Qur'an, which says he didn't die on the cross. So either way, the Qur'an is discredited.

"The bottom line is this: Unless you're a Muslim

who is already committed to the Qur'an, no historian
worth his salt would ever place the Qur'an as a more
credible source on Jesus over the New Testament,
which has four biographies and other writings dated
shortly after Jesus and which contain eyewitness testimony. In historical Jesus studies, I don't know of a
single scholar who consults the Qur'an as a source on
the historical Jesus."

"But it would be hard to prove or disprove whether
Allah substituted somebody at the last minute on the
cross," I said.

"Listen, I could come up with a theory that says we
were all created just five minutes ago with food in our
stomachs from meals we never ate and memories in
our minds of events that never took place. How would
you disprove that? But the question is: Where does the
evidence point? What seems to be the most rational
belief?"

"When I heard a Muslim debate this issue, he took
the approach that Jesus was on the cross and Allah
made him appear to be dead, even though he wasn't," I
said. "Then he claimed Allah healed Jesus."

"Wouldn't this make Allah a deceiver?" Licona
replied. "We could understand it if he deceived his
enemies who were trying to kill Jesus. But since we
know historically that Jesus' disciples sincerely believed that he had been killed and then his corpse had
been transformed into an immortal body, this makes
God a deceiver of his followers as well. If Jesus never

clarified matters with his disciples, then he deceived them too."

I found Licona's logic convincing. Simply applying the tools of modern historical scholarship quickly disqualifies the Qur'an as a trustworthy text about Jesus, if for no other reason than the book's late dating. Scholars quibble over a difference of just a few years in the dating of the New Testament, whereas the Qur'an didn't come until *six centuries* after the life of Christ. However, I also knew that the Qur'an isn't the only book claiming that Jesus didn't die on the cross.

I picked up *The Jesus Papers* and prepared to question Licona about its eye-opening allegations that seek to refute the crucifixion.

Deconstructing Baigent

"Michael Baigent claims in *The Jesus Papers* that although the Jewish Zealots wanted Jesus crucified, Pontius Pilate was conflicted because Jesus had been telling people to pay their taxes to Rome," I said. Then I read Licona this excerpt:

Pilate was Rome's official representative in Judea, and Rome's main argument with the Jews was that they declined to pay their tax to Caesar. Yet here was a leading Jew—the legitimate king no less—telling his people to pay the tax. How could Pilate try, let alone condemn, such a man who, on the face of it, was supporting Roman policy? Pilate would himself be charged with dereliction of duty should he proceed with the condemnation of such a supporter.[15]

"And so," I continued, "Baigent says Pilate decided to condemn Jesus to placate the Zealots, but he took steps to ensure Jesus would survive so he wouldn't have to report to Rome that he had killed him. Baigent speculates that Jesus had been given medication to induce the appearance of death. In fact, the Gospels indicate Jesus died pretty quickly. Doesn't this undermine your claim that Jesus died on the cross?"

"Honestly, this is just so weak," he said. "First, Baigent claims that aloes or myrrh were used to revive Jesus after his ordeal. If these common herbs could be used to resuscitate and bring back to health a crucified individual who had been horribly scourged, then why in the world aren't we using them today?" he asked. "Why aren't hospitals using them? They would be wonder drugs! Come on—that's ridiculous!

"And the idea that Rome would never crucify someone who was supporting them flies in the face of the facts. Look at Paul—he urged people to obey the governing authorities because God has placed them in charge, yet that didn't stop Rome from executing him!

"Think about it: If Jesus survived the crucifixion, he'd be horribly mutilated and limping. How would that convince the disciples that he's the risen prince of life? That's absurd. Baigent has nothing to back up his wild claims. There's a tidal wave of scholarship on the other side."

"Baigent claims the Bible itself backs up his theory," I pointed out. "He says that in Mark, when Joseph of Arimathea requests Jesus' body from Pilate, he uses the Greek word *soma*, which denotes a living body. In reply, Pilate uses the word *ptoma* for body, which means a corpse. Says Baigent: 'In other words, the Greek text of Mark's Gospel is making it clear that while Joseph is asking for the living body of Jesus, Pilate grants him what he believes to be the corpse. *Jesus' survival is revealed right there in the actual Gospel account.*'"[16]

"That's pure rubbish," Licona replied. "The truth is that the word *soma* makes no distinction between a living or dead body. In fact, in Acts 9:37, Luke talks about the death of Tabitha. After she dies, he says they washed her *soma*, or her body. Obviously, it's a corpse. There's example after example, even in Josephus, of *soma* meaning corpse. So Baigent doesn't know what he's talking about here, either.

"What's more, Baigent is ignoring the context in Mark. The Gospel makes it clear that Jesus was dead. Mark 15:37 says Jesus 'breathed his last'; in Mark 15:45, eyewitnesses confirmed Jesus was dead; and in Mark 15:47–16:1, Mary Magdelene and the other women watch Jesus being buried and return Sunday morning to anoint him. They surely thought he was dead. So there's nothing at all to support Baigent's claims."

Clearly, Baigent's case would be instantly dismissed by any impartial judge—as would the Qu'ran's unsupported claim that Jesus escaped the cross. The fact that he was killed by crucifixion remained unrefuted by any credible counter-argument.

All of which raises the question: Why was it necessary for Jesus to die? The reason, simply put, is the atonement. "There the love and justice of God were mutually satisfied, making it possible for us to be reconciled to the Almighty," explained Erwin Lutzer. "Love wanted to redeem us, but justice demanded that we pay for our sin, which for sinners is impossible. Thus God chose to take the initiative and satisfy His own demands."[17]

Incredibly, the horror of the Roman cross becomes an event of stunning—even magnificent—implications. "The crucifixion of Jesus," declared Lutzer, "was God's finest hour so far as we sinners are concerned."[18]

CHAPTER 5

PORTRAIT #5:
THE DECEASED JESUS

Are Stories of His Resurrection
Fabricated?

It was a rare opportunity: there I was, sitting across from *Playboy* founder Hugh Hefner in his opulent Los Angeles mansion, discussing spiritual issues for a television show I was hosting. Hefner, clad in his trademark pajamas and silk smoking jacket, professed a minimal belief in God, as a word for "the beginning of it all" and the "great unknown." But the God of Christianity, he said, was "a little too childlike for me."

Interestingly, when I brought up Jesus' resurrection, Hefner immediately recognized its significance. "If one had any real evidence that, indeed, Jesus did return from the dead, then that is the beginning of a dropping of a series of dominoes that takes us to all kinds of wonderful things," he told me. "It assures an afterlife and all kinds of things that we would all hope are true."

But even though he admitted he had never researched the historical evidence for Jesus returning to life, Hefner remained a doubter. "Do I think that Jesus was the Son of God?" he asked. "I don't think that he is any more the Son of God than we are."

Hefner was right about one thing: everything hinges on the resurrection. If it's true, it confirms Jesus' identity as the unique Son of God and opens the door for eternal life to his followers. If it's a legend or mistake, then Jesus is just another unfortunate crucifixion victim in a long line of revolutionaries and false messiahs.

As I described in the previous chapter, attacks on the resurrection have been mounting in recent years. "Only one conclusion is justified by the evidence: Jesus is dead," said atheist Richard C. Carrier.[1] Robert M. Price, a member of the left-wing Jesus Seminar, concurs. "Jesus is dead," he declared.[2]

Explained retired Episcopal bishop John Shelby Spong: "Jesus was placed into a common grave, and covered over. In a very short time only some unmarked bones remained. Even the bones were gone before too long. Nature rather efficiently reclaims its own resources."[3]

Is Spong's vivid picture accurate? Or are there solid historical reasons for believing Jesus conquered the grave? I decided to seek answers from Michael Licona, the noted resurrection expert who has debated Carrier, Muslim apologist Shabir Ally, agnostic Bart Ehrman, and other resurrection opponents. Licona and resurrection scholar Gary Habermas authored *The Case for the Resurrection of Jesus*, an award-winning book that historian Paul Maier called "the most comprehensive treatment of the subject anywhere."[4]

Getting Past Prejudices

"You can't deny that you see the historical evidence through the lenses of your own prejudices," I said to Licona as we sat in my family room.

"Absolutely. Nobody is exempt, including theists, deists, atheists, or whatever—we all have our biases and there's no way to overcome them," Licona said. "That's why you have to put certain checks and balances in place. This is what historian Gary Habermas did in creating what's called the 'minimal facts approach' to the resurrection."

"How does this keep biases in check?"

"Under this approach, we only consider facts that meet two criteria. First, there must be very strong historical evidence supporting them. And secondly, the evidence must be so strong that the vast majority of today's scholars on the subject—including skeptical ones—accept these as historical facts."

"History isn't a vote," I interjected. "Are you saying people should accept these facts just because a lot of scholars do?"

"No, we're saying that this evidence is so good that even skeptical scholars are convinced by it. Let's face it: there's a greater likelihood that a purported historical fact is true when someone accepts it even though they're not in agreement with your metaphysical beliefs."

"How do you know what these scholars believe?"

"Habermas has compiled a list of more than 2,200

sources in French,.German, and English in which experts have written on the resurrection from 1975 to the present. He has identified minimal facts that are strongly evidenced and which are regarded as historical by the large majority of scholars, including skeptics. We try to come up with the best historical explanation to account for these facts."

With that background in place, I invited Licona to build the case for Jesus rising from the dead. "I'll use just five minimal facts," he said, "and you can decide for yourself how persuasive the case is."

FACT #1: JESUS WAS KILLED BY CRUCIFIXION

I described Licona's evidence supporting this first fact—including multiple sources in the New Testament and five non-Christian sources—in the previous chapter. "Lee, this first fact is as solid as anything in ancient history," said Licona. "The scholarly consensus—again, even among those who are skeptical toward the resurrection—is absolutely overwhelming."

FACT #2: JESUS' DISCIPLES BELIEVED THAT HE ROSE AND APPEARED TO THEM

"The second fact is the disciples' belief that Jesus had actually returned from the dead and had appeared to them," Licona said. "There are three strands of evidence for this: Paul's testimony about the disciples, oral traditions that passed through the early church, and the written works of the early church.

"Paul is important because he reports knowing some of the disciples personally, including Peter, James, and John. Acts confirms this.[5] And Paul says in First Corinthians 15:11 that whether 'it was I or they, this is what we preach,' referring to the resurrection of Jesus. So in other words, Paul knew the apostles and reports that they claimed—just as he did—that Jesus had returned from the dead.

"Then we have oral tradition. Obviously, people in those days didn't have tape recorders and few people could read, so they relied on verbal transmission for passing along what happened until it was later written down. Scholars have identified several places in which this oral tradition has been copied into the New Testament in the form of creeds, hymns, and sermon summations. This is really significant because the oral tradition must have existed prior to the New Testament writings for the New Testament authors to have included them."

"So it's early."

"Very early, which weighs heavily in their favor. For example, we have creeds that laid out basic doctrines in a form that was easily memorized. One of the earliest and most important creeds was relayed by Paul in his first letter to the Corinthian church, which was written about AD 55. It says:

> For I delivered to you as of first importance what I also received, that Christ died for our sins according to the Scriptures, and that he was buried, and that he was raised on the third day according to the Scriptures, and that he appeared to Cephas [Peter], then to the twelve. After that, he appeared to more than five hundred of the brothers at the same time, most of whom are still living, though some have fallen asleep. Then he appeared to James, then to all the apostles....[6]

"Many scholars believe Paul received this creed from Peter and James while visiting with them in Jerusalem three years after his conversion. That would be within five years of the crucifixion. As one expert said, 'This is the sort of data that historians of antiquity drool over.'[7] Not only is it extremely early, but it was apparently given to Paul by eyewitnesses or others he deemed reliable, which heightens its credibility even more."

"How important is this creed?"

"It's powerful and persuasive," he declared. "Although early dating does not totally rule out the possibility of invention or deceit on the part of Jesus' followers, it is much too early to be the result of legendary development over time, since it can practically be traced to the original disciples of Jesus. In fact, this creed has been one of the most formidable obstacles to critics who try to shoot down the resurrection.

"And we've got even more oral tradition—for instance, the New Testament preserves several sermons of the apostles. Actually, these are apparently summaries of the preaching. At a minimum, we can say that the vast majority of historians believe that the early apostolic teachings are enshrined in these sermon summaries in Acts — and they declare that Jesus rose bodily from the dead.

"For example, Paul says in Acts 13, which is very similar to what Peter reports in Acts 2: 'For when David had served God's purpose in his own generation, he fell asleep; he was buried with his ancestors and his body decayed. But the one whom God raised from the dead did not undergo decay.'[8] That's a bold assertion: David's body decayed, but Jesus' didn't, because he was raised from the dead.

"Finally, we have written sources such as Matthew, Mark, Luke, and John. It's widely accepted, even among skeptical historians, that the Gospels were written in the first century. Even very liberal scholars will concede that we have four biographies written within seventy years of Jesus' life that unambiguously report the disciples' claims that Jesus rose from the dead.

"I think an excellent case can be made for dating the Gospels earlier, but let's go with the more generous estimations. That's still extremely close to the events themselves, especially compared to many other ancient historical writings. Our two best sources on Alexander the Great, for instance, weren't written until at least four hundred years after his life.

"Then we have the writings of the apostolic fathers, who were said to have known the apostles or were close to others who did. There's a strong likelihood that their writings reflect the teachings of the apostles themselves—and what do they say? That the apostles were dramatically impacted by Jesus' resurrection.

"Consider Clement, for example. The early church father Irenaeus reports that Clement had conversed with the apostles. Tertullian, the African church father, said Clement was ordained by Peter himself."

"So what does Clement report about the disciples?" I asked.

"In his letter to the Corinthian church, written in the first century, he writes: 'Therefore, having received ... complete certainty caused by the resurrection of our Lord Jesus Christ ... they went ... preaching the good news that the kingdom of God is about to come.'[9]

"Then we have Polycarp. Irenaeus says that Polycarp was 'instructed by the apostles, and conversed with many who had seen Christ,' including John. Tertullian confirms that John appointed Polycarp as bishop of the church in Smyrna. Around AD 110, Polycarp wrote a letter to the Philippian church in which he mentions the resurrection of Jesus no fewer than five times.

"So think about the depth of evidence we have in these three categories: Paul, oral tradition, and written reports. In all, we've got nine sources that reflect multiple, very early, and eyewitness testimonies to the disciples' claims that they had seen the risen Jesus. This is something the disciples believed to the core of their being."

"How do you know that?"

"Because we have evidence that the disciples had been transformed to the point where they were willing to endure persecution and even martyrdom. Just read through Acts and you'll see how the disciples were willing to suffer for their conviction that Jesus rose from the dead. The church fathers Clement, Polycarp, Ignatius, Tertullian, and Origen—they all confirm this. In fact, we've got at least seven early sources testifying that the disciples willingly suffered in defense of their beliefs—and if we include the martyrdoms of Paul and Jesus' half-brother James, we have eleven sources."

"But," I objected, "people of other faiths have been willing to die for their beliefs through the ages—so what does the martyrdom of the disciples really prove?"

"First, it means that they certainly regarded their beliefs to be true," he said. "They didn't willfully lie about this. Liars make poor martyrs. Second, the disciples didn't just *believe* Jesus rose from the dead; they knew for a fact that he did. They were on the scene and able to ascertain for sure that he had been resurrected. So it was for the *truth* of the resurrection that they were willing to die.

"This is totally different from a modern-day Islamic terrorist or others willing to die for their beliefs. These people can only have faith that their beliefs are true, but they aren't in a position to know for sure. The disciples, on the other hand, knew for a *fact* whether the resurrection had truly occurred—and knowing the *truth*, they were willing to die for the belief that they had."

"Then what's the bottom line?" I asked.

"Habermas completed an overview of more than two thousand scholarly sources on the resurrection going back thirty years—and probably no fact was more widely recognized than that the early Christian believers had real experiences that they thought were appearances of the risen Jesus," Licona replied. "Even the atheist Lüdemann conceded: 'It may be taken as historically certain that Peter and the disciples had experiences after Jesus' death in which Jesus appeared to them as the risen Christ.'[10] Now, he claims this was the result of visions, which I simply don't believe is a credible explanation. But he's conceding that their experiences actually occurred."

Licona also cited liberal scholar Paula Fredriksen of Boston University, who said, "The disciples' conviction that they had seen the risen Christ ... is [part of] historical bedrock, facts known past doubting."[11]

"I think that's pretty much undeniable," said Licona. "And I believe the evidence is clear and convincing that what they saw was the return of Jesus from the dead."

FACT #3: THE CONVERSION OF THE CHURCH PERSECUTOR, PAUL

"We know from multiple sources that Paul—then known as Saul of Tarsus—was an enemy of the church and committed to persecuting the faithful," Licona continued. "But Paul himself says that he was converted to a follower of Jesus because he had personally encountered the resurrected Jesus.[12] So we have Jesus' resurrection attested by friend and foe alike, which is very significant.

"Then we have six ancient sources in addition to Paul—Luke, Clement of Rome, Polycarp, Tertullian, Dionysius of Corinth, and Origen—reporting that Paul was willing to suffer continuously and even die for his beliefs. Again, liars make poor martyrs. So we can be confident that Paul not only claimed the risen Jesus appeared to him, but that he really believed it.

"You can't claim that Paul was a friend of Jesus who was primed to see a vision of him due to wishful thinking or grief after his crucifixion. His mindset was to oppose the Christian movement that he believed was following a false Messiah. His radical transformation from persecutor to missionary demands an explanation—and I think the best explanation is that he's telling the truth when he says he met the risen Jesus.

"He had nothing to gain in this world—except his own suffering and martyrdom—for making this up."

FACT #4: THE CONVERSION OF THE SKEPTIC JAMES, JESUS' HALF-BROTHER

"The next minimal fact involves James, the half-brother of Jesus," Licona said. "In the second century,

Hegesippus reports that James was a pious Jew who strictly abided by the Jewish law. But more significantly for our purposes, we also have good evidence that James was not a follower of Jesus during Jesus' lifetime. Mark and John both report that none of Jesus' brothers believed in him."[13]

These reports are most likely true, he said, because "people are not going to invent a story that's going to be embarrassing or potentially discrediting to them, and it would be particularly humiliating for a first-century rabbi not to have his own family as his followers.

"Then, however, the pivotal moment occurs: the ancient creedal material in First Corinthians 15 tells us that the risen Jesus appeared to James. Again, this is an extremely early account that has all the earmarks of reliability. In fact, James may have been involved in passing along this creed to Paul, in which case James would be personally endorsing what the creed reports about him.

"As a result of his encounter with the risen Jesus, James doesn't just become a Christian; he later becomes leader of the Jerusalem church.[14] Actually, James was so thoroughly convinced of Jesus' messiahship because of the resurrection that he died as a martyr, as both Christian and non-Christian sources attest.[15]

"So here we have another example of a skeptic who was converted because of a personal encounter with the resurrected Lord and was willing to die for his convictions."

FACT #5: JESUS' TOMB WAS EMPTY

"Although the fifth fact—that the tomb of Jesus was empty—is part of the minimal case for the resurrection, it doesn't enjoy the nearly universal consensus among scholars that the first four do," Licona began.

"Still, there's strong evidence in its favor. Habermas determined that about seventy-five percent of scholars on the subject regard it as a historical fact. Personally, I think the empty tomb is very well-supported if the historical data are assessed without preconceptions. Basically, there are three strands of evidence: the Jerusalem factor, enemy attestation, and the testimony of women."

"Jerusalem factor?" I asked.

"This refers to the fact that Jesus was publicly executed and buried in Jerusalem and then his resurrection was proclaimed in the very same city. In fact, several weeks after the crucifixion, Peter declares to a crowd in Jerusalem: 'God has raised this Jesus to life, and we are all witnesses of the fact.'[16] Frankly, it would have been impossible for Christianity to get off the ground in Jerusalem if Jesus' body were still in the tomb. The Roman or Jewish authorities could have simply gone over to his tomb, viewed his corpse, and the misunderstanding would have been over.

"Instead, what we do hear is enemy attestation to the empty tomb. In other words, what were the skeptics saying? That the disciples stole the body. This is reported not only by Matthew, but also by Justin Martyr and Tertullian. Here's the thing: Why would you say someone stole the body if it were still in the tomb? This is an implicit admission that the tomb was empty.

"On top of that, the idea that the disciples stole the body is a lame explanation. Are we supposed to believe they conspired to steal the body, pulled it off, and then were willing to suffer continuously and even die for what they knew was a lie? That's such an absurd idea that scholars universally reject it today. In addition, we have the testimony of women that the tomb was empty."

"Why is this important?"

"Because in both first-century Jewish and Roman cultures, women were lowly esteemed and their testimony was considered very questionable. If you were going to concoct a story in an effort to fool others, you would never in that day have hurt your own credibility by saying that women discovered the empty tomb. It would be extremely unlikely that the Gospel writers would invent testimony like this, because they wouldn't get any mileage out of it. In fact, it could hurt them. If they had felt the freedom simply to make things up, surely they'd claim that men — maybe Peter or John — were the first to find the tomb empty.

"The best theory for why the Gospel writers would include such an embarrassing detail is because that's what actually happened and they were committed to recording it accurately, regardless of the credibility problem it created in that culture.

"So when you consider the Jerusalem factor, the

enemy attestation, and the testimony of women, there are good historical reasons for concluding Jesus' tomb was empty. William Ward of Oxford University put it this way: 'All the strictly historical evidence we have is in favor [of the empty tomb], and those scholars who reject it ought to recognize that they do so on some other ground than that of scientific history.'"[17]

"Okay, how would you summarize your case?"

"Shortly after Jesus died from crucifixion, his disciples believed that they saw him risen from the dead. They said he appeared not only to individuals but in several group settings—and the disciples were so convinced and transformed by the experience that they were willing to suffer and even die for their conviction that they had encountered him.

"Then we have two skeptics who regarded Jesus as a false prophet—Paul, the persecutor of the church, and James, who was Jesus' half-brother. They completely changed their opinions 180 degrees after encountering the risen Jesus. Like the disciples, they were willing to endure hardship, persecution, and even death rather than disavow their testimony that Jesus' resurrection occurred.

"Thus we have compelling testimony about the resurrection from friends of Jesus, an enemy of Christianity, and a skeptic. Finally, we have strong historical evidence that Jesus' tomb was empty. In fact, even enemies of Christianity admitted it was vacant. Where did the body go? If you asked the disciples, they'd tell you they personally saw Jesus after he returned to life.

"What's the best explanation for the evidence—the explanation that doesn't leave out any of the facts or strains to make anything fit? My conclusion, based on the evidence, is that Jesus did return from the dead. No other explanation comes close to accounting for all of the facts. Historically speaking, I think we've got a cogent and convincing case."

Dying and Rising Gods

One popular claim is that Christianity stole its belief about the resurrection from earlier pagan stories about dying and rising gods. Why, I asked Licona, should the account of Jesus' resurrection have any more credibility than these obviously mythological tales?

"First, it's important to understand that these claims don't in any way negate the good historical evidence we have for Jesus' resurrection," he pointed out. "Second, T.N.D. Mettinger—a senior Swedish scholar, professor at Lund University and member of the Royal Academy of Letters, History, and Antiquities of Stockholm—wrote one of the most recent academic treatments of dying and rising gods in antiquity. He admits in *The Riddle of Resurrection* that the consensus among modern scholars—*nearly universal*—is that there were no dying and rising gods that preceded Christianity. They all post-dated the first century."

Obviously, Christianity couldn't have borrowed the idea of the resurrection if these myths weren't circulating when Christianity was birthed.

"Then Mettinger said he was going to take exception to that nearly universal scholarly conviction," Licona continued. "He takes a decidedly minority position and claims that there are at least three and possibly as many as five dying and rising gods that predate Christianity. But the key question is: Are there any actual parallels between these myths and Jesus' resurrection?

"In the end, after combing through all of these accounts and critically analyzing them, Mettinger adds that none of these serve as parallels to Jesus. *None* of them," Licona emphasized. "They are far different from the reports of Jesus rising from the dead. They occurred in the unspecified and distant past and were usually related to the seasonal life-and-death cycle of vegetation. In contrast, Jesus' resurrection isn't repeated, isn't related to changes in the seasons, and was sincerely believed to be an actual event by those who lived in the same generation of the historical Jesus. In addition, Mettinger concludes that 'there is no evidence for the death of the dying and rising gods as vicarious suffering for sins.' "[18]

Mettinger caps his study with this stunning statement: "There is, as far as I am aware, no *prima facie* evidence that the death and resurrection of Jesus is a mythological construct, drawing on the myths and rites of the dying and rising gods of the surrounding world."[19] Ultimately, Mettinger affirmed, "the death and resurrection of Jesus retains its unique character in the history of religions."[20]

Accounting for the Data

Licona could have presented all kinds of historical evidence for the resurrection, but instead he limited himself only to five facts that are extremely well-attested and that the vast majority of scholars — including skeptics — concede are trustworthy. I had to agree: the case was cogent and compelling. As historian N. T. Wright, author of *The Resurrection of the Son of God*, put it:

> It is no good falling back on "science" as having disproved the possibility of resurrection. Any real scientist will tell you that science observes what normally happens; the Christian case is precisely that what happened to Jesus is not what normally happens. For my part, as a historian I prefer the elegant, essentially simple solution rather than the one that fails to include all the data: to say that the early Christians believed that Jesus had been bodily raised from the dead, and to account for this belief by saying that they were telling the truth.[21]

CONCLUSION

THE REAL JESUS —FOUND

Not long ago, Craig A. Evans had enough. With righteous indignation, he set out to expose the sloppy scholarship that has confused the public with distorted portraits of Jesus in recent years.

Coming from someone of Evans' impressive caliber, this was highly significant. Few Jesus scholars are as universally respected by both liberals and conservatives as Evans, the distinguished professor of New Testament and director of the graduate program at Acadia Divinity College in Canada and the first expert I interviewed in my quest for the real Jesus.

Evans looked at the current controversies swirling around Jesus—*was he a Gnostic, did he fake his death, are the four Gospels unreliable, are there better sources about his life than the New Testament, is there a grand conspiracy to suppress the truth, did Jesus ever really exist at all?*—and shook his head in disbelief. "Surely no one in all seriousness would advance such theories," he said. "Surely no credible publishers would print them. Yet, all of that has happened."[1]

Evans knows the sweep of historical evidence. He's

well aware of what conclusions it reasonably supports
and what it can't. And he was aghast at what he was
reading in popular books about Jesus.

"We live in a strange time that indulges, even encourages, some of the strangest thinking," he wrote in
*Fabricating Jesus: How Modern Scholars Distort the
Gospels*. "What I find particularly troubling is that a
lot of the nonsense comes from scholars. We expect
tabloid pseudo-scholarship from the quacks, but not
from scholars who teach at respectable institutions of
higher learning."[2]

Nevertheless, what he found were fanciful theories
that run beyond the evidence, distortions or neglect of
the four Gospels, misguided suspicions, unduly strict
critical methods, questionable texts from later centuries, anachronisms, exaggerated claims, and "hokum
history"—all resulting in "the fabrication of an array
of pseudo-Jesuses."[3]

In sum, he said, "Just about every error imaginable
has been made. A few writers have made almost all of
them."[4]

A Chorus of Criticism

Evans isn't alone in his assessment. Numerous other
New Testament luminaries also have started to publicly condemn the way readers are being duped by ill-
supported pictures of Jesus.

James H. Charlesworth, professor of New Testament Language and Literature at Princeton Theological Seminary and an expert on Jesus and the Dead Sea

Scrolls, decried "the misinformed nonsense that has confused the reading public over the past few years."

James D. G. Dunn, professor emeritus at the University of Durham in England, agreed. "The quest of the historical Jesus has been seriously misled by much poor scholarship and distorted almost beyond recognition by recent pseudo-scholarship," he said.

Equally adamant was John P. Meier, professor at the University of Notre Dame and author of a widely acclaimed multivolume work on Jesus. "For decades now," he said, "the unsuspecting public has been subjected to dubious academic claims about the historical Jesus that hardly rise above the level of sensationalistic novels."

Gerald O'Collins, professor emeritus of the Gregorian University in Rome, warned of the "sensationalist claims about Jesus that quickly turn out to be based on mere wishful thinking." Gerd Theissen, professor at the University of Heidelberg, bemoaned "sensational modern approaches in Jesus research that do not live up to the standards of academic research."[5]

"Readers should beware of shocking new claims about Jesus or his earliest followers based on flimsy evidence," warned New Testament professor Ben Witherington III.[6] Unfortunately, he added, Americans have been "prone to listen to sensational claims ... even when there is little or no hard evidence to support such conjectures."[7]

Answering the Challenges

In the end, none of the sensational claims about Jesus that I investigated turned out to be close calls. One by one, they were systematically dismantled by scholars who backed up their positions not with verbal sleights of hand or speculation, but with facts, logic, and evidence:

- *The Gnostic Jesus?* No, the mystical texts touted in liberal circles are too late to be historically credible — for instance, the Gospel of Thomas was written after AD 175 and probably closer to 200. According to eminent New Testament scholar I. Howard Marshall of the University of Aberdeen, the Thomas gospel has "no significant new light to shed on the historical Jesus."[8] The Gnostic depiction of Jesus as a revealer of hidden knowledge — including the teaching that we all possess the divine light that he embodied — lacks any connection to the historical Jesus.
- *The Misquoted Jesus?* No, there are no new disclosures that have cast any doubt on the essential reliability of the text of the New Testament. Only about one percent of the manuscript variants affect the meaning of the text to any degree, and not a single cardinal doctrine is at stake. Actually, the unrivaled wealth of New Testament manuscripts greatly enhances the credibility of the Bible's portrayal of Jesus.
- *The Failed Jesus?* No, Jesus succeeded in fulfilling all of the messianic prophecies that had to have been accomplished prior to the fall of the Jewish

temple in AD 70. Consequently, if Jesus isn't the predicted Messiah, then there will never be one. What's more, his fulfillment of these time-sensitive prophecies makes it rational to conclude that he will fulfill the final ones when the time is right.

- *The Uncrucified Jesus?* No, the historical evidence—both in the New Testament and in sources outside the Bible—clearly confirms that Jesus was dead when he was taken down from the cross. The Qur'an's claim that Jesus wasn't executed simply lacks historical credibility.

- *The Deceased Jesus?* No, a persuasive case for Jesus rising from the dead can be made by using five facts that are well-evidenced and which the vast majority of today's scholars on the subject—including skeptics—accept as true: Jesus was killed by crucifixion; his disciples believed he rose and appeared to them; the conversion of the church persecutor Paul; the conversion of the skeptic James, who was Jesus' half-brother; and Jesus' empty tomb.[9] The best explanation for these facts is that Jesus did, indeed, conquer the grave.

Following the Unique Jesus

Not only had the five portraits been unmasked as phony, but my investigative journey also had yielded a powerful affirmative case for the reliability of the four Gospels, Jesus' fulfillment of the messianic predictions, and his resurrection. For me, it was further confirmation that the traditional view of Christ is amply supported by a firm foundation of historical facts.

In fact, remember the story I told in the introduction about the scientist who challenged me with tough objections to my understanding of Jesus? The rest of the story is this: I went out and investigated each and every one of his charges — only to find time and again that they disintegrated in the face of the historical data.

As it turns out, the real Jesus is the One who has been worshipped for two thousand years: he's the unique Son of God who sacrificed himself on the cross in payment of our sins and who offers forgiveness and eternal life as a free gift that cannot be earned. That's the "good news," or Gospel, which can be summarized by three verses known as the Roman Road. Romans 3:23: "For all have sinned and fall short of the glory of God." Romans 6:23: "For the wages of sin is death, but the gift of God is eternal life in Christ Jesus our Lord." And Romans 10:13: "Everyone who calls on the name of the Lord will be saved."

Some people hesitate to receive Jesus as their forgiver and leader because they think he could demand too much. And the truth is that he does demand everything. Said C. S. Lewis:

> The Christian way is different: harder, and easier. Christ says, "Give me All. I don't want so much of your time and so much of your money and so much of your work: I want You. I have not come to torment your natural self, but to kill it. No half-measures are any good.... Hand over the whole natural self, all the desires which you think innocent as well as the ones you think wicked — the whole outfit. I will

give you a new self instead. In fact, I will give you Myself: my own will shall become yours."[10]

That kind of surrender can sound scary. But if Jesus really is God—if he really did sacrifice himself so that we could be forgiven and set free to experience his love forever—then why should we hesitate to give all of ourselves to him? Who could be more trustworthy than someone who lays down his life so that others might live?

This is what Jesus has done. He is without a doubt one of a kind. "Jesus," said author Don Everts, "was entirely different and new and stunning."

> There was just something so clear and beautiful and true and unique and powerful about Jesus that old rabbis would marvel at his teaching, young children would run and sit in his lap, ashamed prostitutes would find themselves weeping at his feet, whole villages would gather to hear him speak, experts in the law would find themselves speechless, and people from the poor to the rugged working class to the unbelievably wealthy would leave everything ... to follow him.[11]

This is the *real* Jesus, who all along has been alive and well—and fully available to "everyone who calls on the name of the Lord."

RECOMMENDED RESOURCES

Books

Bowman, Robert M. Jr., and J. Ed Komoszewski. *Putting Jesus in His Place*. Grand Rapids: Kregel, 2007.

Brown, Michael L. *Answering Jewish Objections to Jesus*. (Volumes 1–4) Grand Rapids: Baker, 2000–2006.

Evans, Craig A. *Fabricating Jesus*. Downers Grove, Ill.: InterVarsity, 2006.

Habermas, Gary R., and Michael R. Licona. *The Case for the Resurrection of Jesus*. Grand Rapids: Kregel, 2004.

Komoszewski, J. Ed, M. James Sawyer, and Daniel B, Wallace. *Reinventing Jesus*. Grand Rapids: Kregel, 2006.

Nash, Robert H. *The Gospel and the Greeks*. Phillipsburg, N.J.: P&R Publishing, 2003.

Strobel, Lee. *The Case for Christ*. Grand Rapids: Zondervan, 1998.

Strobel, Lee. *The Case for the Real Jesus*. Grand Rapids: Zondervan, 2007.

Websites

LEESTROBEL.COM
... a video-intensive site on what Christians believe—and why.

JESUSCENTRAL.COM
... a place to learn and dialogue about what Jesus said.

REASONABLEFAITH.ORG
... scholar William Lane Craig defends Christianity.

CHRISTIAN-THINKTANK.COM
... a vast resource of answers to objections to Christianity.

TEKTONICS.ORG
... a feisty site that answers critics of Christianity.

METAMORPHA.COM
... focusing on how to become more like Jesus.

NOTES

INTRODUCTION

1. Lee Strobel, "Chicagoan named in federal suit citing World War II crimes against Jews," *Chicago Tribune*, Jan. 27, 1977.
2. Lee Strobel, "Walus turns in citizenship papers," *Chicago Tribune*, July 11, 1978.
3. Dorothy Collin, "Walus is cleared; all hail U.S. justice," *Chicago Tribune*, Nov. 27, 1980.
4. Ibid.
5. See: Lee Strobel, *The Case for Christ* (Grand Rapids: Zondervan, 1998) and *The Case for a Creator* (Grand Rapids: Zondervan, 2004).
6. See: Colossians 1:15.
7. John 1:1, 14a.
8. New Living Translation (emphasis added).
9. First Thessalonians 5:21.

CHAPTER 1:
PORTRAIT #1: THE GNOSTIC JESUS

1. See: N.T. Wright, *Judas and the Gospel of Jesus* (Grand Rapids: Baker, 2006), 31–34.
2. Ibid., 33.
3. Elaine Pagels, *Beyond Belief: The Secret Gospel of Thomas* (New York: Vintage Books, 2004), 40–41.

4. Jay Tolson, "In Search of the Real Jesus: The Gospel Truth," *U.S. News and World Report*, Dec. 18, 2006.

5. Ben Witherington III, *The Gospel Code* (Downers Grove, Ill.: InterVarsity, 2004), 101.

6. Willis Barnstone and Marvin Meyer, *The Gnostic Bible* (Boston: New Seeds, 2006), 48, 69.

7. Jay Tolson, "In Search of the Real Jesus: The Gospel Truth."

8. Richard Cimino and Don Lattin, *Shopping for Faith* (San Francisco: Jossey-Bass, 1998), 19.

9. Ibid., 19–20.

10. Jay Tolson, "In Search of the Real Jesus: The Gospel Truth."

11. All interviews edited for content, clarity, and conciseness. Interviews condensed from: Lee Strobel, *The Case for the Real Jesus* (Grand Rapids: Zondervan, 2007).

12. Stevan L. Davies, *The Gospel of Thomas and Christian Wisdom* (New York: Seabury, 1983), 146.

13. See: John Dominic Crossan, *The Historical Jesus: The Life of a Mediterranean Jewish Peasant* (San Francisco: HarperCollins, 1991), 427–34.

14. See: Nicholas Perrin, *Thomas and Tatian: The Relationship Between the Gospel of Thomas and the Diatessaron*, Academia Biblica 5 (Atlanta: Society of Biblical Literature, 2002); Nicholas Perrin, "NHC II,2 and the Oxyrhynchus Fragments (P.Oxy 1, 654, 655): Overlooked Evidence for a Syriac Gospel of Thomas," *Vigiliae Christianae* 58 (2004): 138–51; and Nicholas Perrin, *Thomas, the Other Gospel* (Louisville: Westminster John Knox Press, 2007).

15. *Against Heresies* 1.31.1.

CHAPTER 2:
PORTRAIT #2: THE MISQUOTED JESUS

1. Emphasis added.
2. Bart D. Ehrman, *Misquoting Jesus* (New York: HarperOne, 2005), 89–90.
3. Ibid., 7.
4. Ben Witherington III, "Misanalyzing Text Criticism— Bart Ehrman's 'Misquoting Jesus," http://benwitherington .blogspot.com/2006/03/misanalyzing-test-criticism-bart -html (June 6, 2006).
5. See: John 7:53–8:11.
6. Shawntaye Hopkins, "Woman Bitten by Snake at Church Dies," *Lexington (Ky.) Herald-Leader*, Nov. 8, 2006.
7. Frank Zindler, *The Real Bible: Who's Got it?* www .atheists.org/christianity/realbible.html (Nov. 29, 2006).
8. Bart D. Ehrman, *Misquoting Jesus*, Acknowledgements.
9. For the entire interview with Metzger, who died in 2007, see: Lee Strobel, *The Case for Christ* (Grand Rapids: Zondervan, 1998), 55–72.

CHAPTER 3:
PORTRAIT #3: THE FAILED JESUS

1. Aryeh Kaplan, *The Real Messiah?* (Toronto: Jews for Judaism, 2004), 14.
2. See: John 4:25–26.
3. Aryeh Kaplan, *The Real Messiah?*, 16.
4. "Do All Scholars Believe Jesus Fulfilled Messianic Prophecies?" www.whoisthisjesus.tv/qa.htm#scholars (Dec. 28, 2006).
5. Ibid.
6. See: Isaiah 42:4.

7. See: Second Chronicles 7:19–22.

8. See: Daniel 9:24.

9. See: Haggai 2:6–9.

10. See: Malachi 3:1–5.

11. For a description of the time reckoning, see: Michael L. Brown, *Answering Jewish Objections to Jesus*, Vol. 1: *General and Historical Objections* (Grand Rapids: Baker, 2000), 70–71.

12. See: Babylonian Talmud, Sanhedrin 98a.

13. Matthew 27:46 and Mark 15:34 report Jesus saying on the cross, "My God, my God, why have you forsaken me?" This is the first line of Psalm 22. In Jesus' day, the Psalms were not numbered; people referred to them by their opening line.

14. See Psalm 22:27–31.

15. See: Deuteronomy 18:15–22.

16. Torah, which means "teaching, instruction, law," can refer to the first division of the Tanakh (the Old Testament) or the Oral Torah, which is composed of all rabbinic traditions related to the Written Torah and various legal aspects of the Jewish life. The traditions were first passed on orally before they were written down. See: Michael L. Brown, *Answering Jewish Objections to Jesus*, vol. 1: *General and Historical Objections*, 255–56.

17. See: Isaiah 53:10.

18. See: Babylonian Talmud, Yoma 39a.

19. Ibid.

20. First Peter 2:24: "He himself bore our sins in his body on the tree, so that we might die to sins and live for righteousness; by his wounds you have been healed."

CHAPTER 4:
PORTRAIT #4: THE UNCRUCIFIED JESUS

1. "'Islamic Jesus' hits Iranian movie screens," www.arab timesonline.com/client/pagesdetails.asp?nid=10722 &ccid=18 (Jan. 13, 2008).
2. See Surah 4:157–158.
3. "Who Is the True Jesus?" videotape, available at: http://www.facultylinc.com/national/fslf.nsf (Oct. 1, 2006).
4. Hassan M. Fattah, "In Qaeda Video, Zawahri Condemns Bush and Pope Benedict," *New York Times*, Sept. 30, 2006.
5. Lemuel Lall, "Jesus Christ Lived in India, was buried in Kashmir: RSS Chief," www.hindustantimes.com/news/5922_1914198,0015002100000000.htm (Jan. 28, 2007).
6. Michael Baigent, *The Jesus Papers* (San Francisco: HarperSanFrancisco, 2006), 125.
7. See: Ibid., 124–32.
8. First Corinthians 15:17.
9. John Dominic Crossan, *Jesus: A Revolutionary Biography* (San Francisco: HarperCollins, 1991), 145.
10. James D. Tabor, *The Jesus Dynasty* (New York: Simon & Schuster, 2006), 230 (emphasis in original).
11. See: Deuteronomy 21:23.
12. Abdullah Yusuf Ali, translator, *The Qur'an* (Elmhurst, NY: Tahrike Tarsile Qur'an, Inc., 1999), 61.
13. *The True Furqan* (Duncanville, TX: World Wide Printing, 2006). This is not to say that pure Christian doctrine is presented in *The True Furqan*. One could write it using any doctrine, true or false, and it could still serve to answer the test presented in the Qur'an.
14. Abdullah Yusuf Ali, translator, *The Qur'an*, 1.
15. Michael Baigent, *The Jesus Papers*, 125.
16. Ibid., 130 (emphasis added).

17. Erwin Lutzer, *Slandering Jesus* (Carol Stream, Ill.: Tyndale, 2007), 50–51.
18. Ibid., 50.

CHAPTER 5:
PORTRAIT #5: THE DECEASED JESUS

1. Richard C. Carrier, "The Spiritual Body of Christ and the Legend of the Empty Tomb," in: Robert M. Price and Jeffrey Jay Lowder, editors, *The Empty Tomb* (Amberst, N.Y.: Prometheus Books, 2005), 197.
2. Robert M. Price and Jeffery Jay Lowder, editors, *The Empty Tomb*, 16.
3. John Shelby Spong, *Resurrection: Myth or Reality?* (San Francisco: HarperSanFrancisco, 1995), 241.
4. Gary R. Habermas and Michael R. Licona, *The Case for the Resurrection of Jesus* (Grand Rapids: Kregel, 2004), 1.
5. See: Acts 9:26–30; 15:1–35.
6. First Corinthians 15:3–7.
7. Dean John Rodgers of Trinity Episcopal School for Ministry, quoted in: Richard N. Ostling, "Who was Jesus?" *Time*, August 15, 1988.
8. See: Acts 13:36–39.
9. First Clement 42:3.
10. Gerd Lüdemann, *What Really Happened to Jesus?* (John Bowden, translator) (Louisville: Westminster John Knox, 1995), 80.
11. Paula Fredriksen, *Jesus of Nazareth* (New York: Vintage, 1999), 264.
12. See: First Corinthians 9:1 and 15:8; Acts 9, 22, and 26.
13. See: Mark 3:21, 31; 6:3–4; and John 7:3–5.
14. See: Acts 15:12–21; and Galatians 1:19.

15. See: Josephus (*Ant.* 20:200); Hegesippus (quoted by Eusebius in *EH* 2:23); Clement of Alexandria (quoted by Eusebius in *EH* 2:1, 23.)

16. Acts 2:32.

17. William Ward, *Christianity: A Historical Religion?* (Valley Forge, Pa.: Judson, 1972), 93–94.

18. Tryggve N.D. Mettinger, *The Riddle of Resurrection* (Stockholm: Almqvist & Wicksell, 2001), 221.

19. Ibid.

20. Ibid.

21. Marcus Borg and N. T. Wright, *The Meaning of Jesus: Two Visions* (San Francisco: HarperSanFrancisco, 1999), 124–125.

CONCLUSION:
THE REAL JESUS—FOUND

1. Craig A. Evans, *Fabricating Jesus: How Modern Scholars Distort the Gospels* (Downers Grove, Ill.: InterVarsity, 2006), 15.

2. Ibid., 15–16.

3. Ibid., 16.

4. Ibid.

5. Quotes by Charlesworth, Dunn, Meier, O'Collins, and Theissen are found in the opening, unnumbered pages of: Craig A. Evans' *Fabricating Jesus: How Modern Scholars Distort the Gospels.*

6. Ben Witherington III, *What Have They Done with Jesus?* (San Francisco: HarperSanFrancisco, 2006), 1.

7. Ibid., 2.

8. Craig A. Evans, *Fabricating Jesus: How Modern Scholars Distort the Gospels,* from opening, unnumbered pages.

9. While there's a nearly universal consensus among scholars—including skeptics—concerning the first four facts, about seventy-five percent affirm the empty tomb,

according to Gary Habermas' analysis of more than 2,200 scholarly articles on the resurrection written over the last thirty years in German, French, and English.

10. C. S. Lewis, *Mere Christianity* (New York: HarperCollins, revised and amplified edition, 2001), 196–97.

11. Don Everts, *Jesus with Dirty Feet* (Downers Grove, Ill.: InterVarsity, 1999), 26–27.

GET THESE TITLES BY *NEW YORK TIMES* BESTSELLING AUTHOR, LEE STROBEL

The Case for Christ— #1 Bestseller

A Journalist's Personal Investigation of the Evidence for Jesus

Softcover 978-0-310-20930-0

The Case for a Creator

A Journalist Investigates Scientific Evidence That Points Toward God

Softcover 978-0-310-24050-1

The Case for Faith

A Journalist Investigates the Toughest Objections to Christianity

Softcover 978-0-310-23469-2

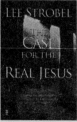

The Case for the Real Jesus

A Journalist Investigates Current Attacks on the Identity of Christ

Softcover 978-0-310-28608-0